SPARKNOTES

Power Tactics

FOR THE NEW SAT

THE WRITING SECTION
THE ESSAY

SPARK
NOTES

A DIVISION OF BARNES & NOBLE PUBLISHING

SPARKNOTES is a registered trademark of SparkNotes LLC

Spark Educational Publishing
A Division of Barnes & Noble Publishing
120 Fifth Avenue
New York, NY 10011

ISBN 1-4114-0274-X

Please submit changes or report errors to *www.sparknotes.com/errors*

Printed and bound in Canada.

SAT is the registered trademark of the College Entrance Examination Board, which was not involved in the production of, and does not endorse, this product.

Written by Doug Tarnopol

CONTENTS

INTRODUCTION

Truly effective SAT preparation doesn't need to be painful or time-consuming. SparkNotes' *Power Tactics for the New SAT* is proof that powerful test preparation can be streamlined so that you study only what you need. Instead of toiling away through a 700-page book or an expensive six-week course, you can choose the *Power Tactics* book that gets you where you want to be a lot sooner.

Perhaps you're Kid Math, the fastest number-slinger this side of the Mississippi, but a bit of a bumbler when it comes to words. Or maybe you've got the verbal parts down but can't seem to manage algebraic functions. SparkNotes' *Power Tactics for the New SAT* provides an extremely focused review of every component on the new SAT, so you can design your own program of study.

If you're not exactly sure where you fall short, log on to **testprep.sparknotes.com/powertactics** and take our free diagnostic SAT test. This test will pinpoint your weaknesses and reveal exactly where to focus.

Since you're holding this book in your hands, it's pretty likely that the SAT essay is giving you trouble. You've made the right decision, because in a few short hours, you will have mastered this part of the exam. No sweat, no major investment of time or money, no problem.

So, let's not waste any time. go forth and conquer the SAT essay so you can get on with the *better parts* of your life!

ABOUT THE NEW SAT

THE OLD

The SAT, first administered in 1926, has undergone a thorough restructuring. For the last ten years, the SAT consisted of two sections: Verbal and Math. The Verbal section contained Analogies, Sentence Completions, and Critical Reading passages and questions. The Math section tested arithmetic, algebra, and geometry, as well as some probability, statistics, and data interpretation.

You received one point for each correct answer. For most questions, a quarter of a point was deducted for each incorrect answer. This was called the "wrong-answer penalty," which was designed to neutralize random guessing. If you simply filled in the bubble sheet at random, you'd likely get one-fifth of the items correct, given that each item has five answer choices (excluding student-produced–response items). You'd also get four-fifths of the items wrong, losing $4 \times {}^1/_4$, or 1 point for the four incorrectly answered items. Every time you determined an answer choice was wrong, you'd improve your odds by beating the wrong-answer penalty. The net number of points (less wrong-answer penalties) was called the "raw score."

Raw score = # of correct answers – (${}^1/_4$ × # of wrong answers)

That score was then converted to the familiar 200–800 "scaled score."

THE NEW

For 2005, the SAT added a Writing section and an essay, changed the name of *Verbal* to *Critical Reading*, and added algebra II content to the Math section. The following chart compares the old SAT with the new SAT:

Old SAT	New SAT
Verbal	**Critical Reading**
Analogies	*Eliminated*
Sentence Completions	Sentence Completions
Long Reading Passages	Long Reading Passages
Paired Reading Passages	Paired Reading Passages
	Short Reading Passages
Math—Question Types	
Multiple Choice	Multiple Choice
Quantitative Comparisons	*Eliminated*
Student-produced Responses	Student-produced Responses
Math—Content Areas	
Numbers & Operations	Numbers & Operations
Algebra I	Algebra I
	Algebra II
Geometry	Geometry
Data Analysis, Statistics & Probability	Data Analysis, Statistics & Probability
	Writing
	Identifying Sentence Errors
	Improving Sentences
	Improving Paragraphs
	Essay
Total Time: 3 hours	*Total Time*: 3 hours, 45 minutes
Maximum Scaled Score: 1600	*Maximum Scaled Score*: 2400 Separate Essay Score (2–12)

The scoring for the test is the same, except that the Writing section provides a third 200–800 scaled score, and there is now a separate essay score. The wrong-answer penalty is still in effect.

NEW PACKAGE, OLD PRODUCT

While the test has changed for test-*takers*, it has not changed all that much from the test-*maker*'s point of view. The Educational Testing Service (ETS) is a not-for-profit institute that creates the SAT for The College Board. Test creation is not as simple a task as you might think. Any standardized test question has to go through a rigorous series of editorial reviews and statistical studies before it can be released to the public. In fact, that's why the old SAT featured a seventh unscored, "experimental" section: new questions were introduced and tested out in these sections. ETS "feeds" potential questions to its test-takers in order to measure the level of difficulty. Given the complex and lengthy process of developing new questions, it would be impossible for ETS to introduce *totally* new question types or make major changes to existing question types.

Now that you know these facts, the "new" SAT will start to make more sense. The changes were neither random nor unexpected. Actually, the only truly *new* question type on the SAT is the short reading passage followed by a couple of questions. However, the skills tested and strategies required are virtually identical to the tried-and-true long reading-passage question type. All other additions to the test consist of new *content* rather than new *question types*. Both multiple-choice and student-produced–response math questions ("grid-ins") will now feature algebra II concepts. Same question type, new content. Critical Reading features one fiction passage per test, as well as questions on genre, rhetorical devices, and cause and effect. Same question type, different content.

Even the much-feared new Writing section is in a sense old news. The PSAT and the SAT II Writing tests have featured exactly the same multiple-choice question types for years. The essay format and scoring rubric are virtually identical to those of the SAT II Writing test. The College Board had no other choice, given how long the test-development process is.

The other major changes are omissions, not additions: Quantitative Comparisons and Analogies have been dumped from the test.

So, in a nutshell, ETS has simply attached an SAT II Writing test to the old SAT, dropped Analogies and Quantitative Comparisons, added some algebra II content and short reading passages, and ensured that some fiction and fiction-related questions are included. That's it.

A USER'S GUIDE

Reading this book will maximize your score on the new SAT essay. Writing—even SAT essay writing—is a complex task, so we provide you with concrete, targeted tools to master this part of the new SAT. We've divided up your study of the essay into two sections: **Power Tactics** and **Practice Sets**. The Power Tactics will provide you with important concepts and strategies you'll need to tackle the SAT essay. The Practice Sets will give you an opportunity to apply what you learn to SAT essay prompts.

To achieve your target score, you'll learn:

- The format of the essay, including what the real essay prompts and assignments look like
- About the scoring rubric, and how to use it to your advantage
- Essential concepts and a powerful step method to maximize your score
- The 15 most common mistakes and how to avoid them

In order to get the most out of this book:

- Make sure to read each section thoroughly and carefully.
- Don't skip the Slow Motion essay experience.
- Read all sample essays and explanations.
- Go to **testprep.sparknotes.com/powertactics** for a free full-length diagnostic **pretest**. This test will help you determine your strengths and weaknesses for the Writing section and for the entire SAT.
- Go back to our website after you complete this book to submit an essay for **grading**.

Like any kind of physical activity, such as weightlifting or dancing, a mental activity like mastering the SAT essay can be quite challenging. The rewards, however, are as great as the challenges. Look upon this book as your personal trainer. If you stick with the program, you'll reach your full potential.

THE POWER
TACTICS

ANATOMY OF THE SAT ESSAY

Yes, it's true: the SAT now has an essay. It's part of the Writing section, and you'll have 25 minutes to complete it.

Before we get into the concepts and strategies you'll use to tackle the essay, let's lay out the terrain. In this section, we provide you with an X-ray of the SAT essay by answering the following questions:

- What does the essay look like?
- What skills does the essay test?
- Who creates the essay prompts?
- Who scores the essay?
- How is the essay scored?
- The bigger picture: how does the essay figure into the entire SAT score?

Answering these questions will not only demystify the SAT but will also put you in a good position to prepare yourself for writing a winning essay.

You may be asking yourself, "Why do I need to know so much about the essay score? I'm *writing* the essay, not scoring it." Well, understanding how to score the SAT essay will actually help you to write a better essay. By studying the scoring process in detail, you'll understand exactly what your writing should include and what you should avoid. Most important, you'll gain an understanding of how The College Board defines good writing, which is not necessarily how you, your teachers, or your parents may define it.

WHAT DOES THE ESSAY LOOK LIKE?

What follows is a testlike example of a Student Response Sheet. We've inserted numbered boxes that comment on each part of the Student Response Sheet. Match up these numbers to the explanations on pages 14–15.

Student Response Sheet
Page 1 of 4

Essay scores range
from 2 to 12.
Scores of 7 and 8
are average.
Your score is

2

Name _____

1 Teacher/School _____

Signature _____ Date ___ / ___ / ___

3 You have 25 minutes to plan and write an essay on the topic assigned below.

4 Make sure you express your ideas clearly and effectively. Cover the topic as thoroughly and specifically as you can, supporting your ideas with evidence.

5 You may use the blank space beneath the topic to plan your essay, but please write your essay on the lined pages of the response sheet. You will have enough space if you write all the way across every line and keep your handwriting reasonably sized. **6** You may use either a pen or a pencil. **7** Try to write or print so that what you are writing is easily understood by the reader. **8** You will have space underneath the assignment to note your initial thoughts. **9** Use of scrap paper is not allowed.

10 **DO NOT WRITE ON ANOTHER TOPIC.**
AN ESSAY ON ANOTHER TOPIC IS UNACCEPTABLE.

When you are told to do so, turn over your response sheet.

Student Response Sheet
Page 2 of 4

Essay Prompt:

Think carefully about the issue presented in the quotations and the assignment below.

1.   Technological progress, while often beneficial, has nevertheless outpaced human social and ethical development. We lack the wisdom to manage these increasingly dangerous tools.

                        —Adapted from Hugh B. Riis, "Techno-hazard"

2.   The past four centuries have seen the greatest improvement of the human condition in history. Technological progress, while not without its pitfalls, holds out the possibility of achieving a healthier and more humane society in which people lead richer and longer lives than were ever thought possible.

                        —Editorial, "Technology: The Way Forward"

Assignment: Is technology dangerous or does it provide a way to solve our problems? Plan and write an essay in which you develop your position on this issue. Support your point of view with reasoning and examples taken from your reading, studies, experience, or observations.

Student Response Sheet
Page 3 of 4

START YOUR ESSAY ON THIS SIDE. YOU MAY CONTINUE ON THE REVERSE SIDE
IF YOU NEED MORE SPACE.

IF NECESSARY, CONTINUE YOUR ESSAY ON THE REVERSE SIDE.

Student Response Sheet
Page 4 of 4

CONTINUATION OF ESSAY FROM REVERSE SIDE. WRITE ON THIS SHEET ONLY
IF YOU NEED MORE SPACE.

Last Name
First 2 letters

DO NOT WRITE BELOW.

Score

First Reader _____   Recorded by _____

Second Reader _____   Recorded by _____

1. Biographical information, signature, and date go here.
2. Your score will be written here.
3. Instructions—note it says *plan and write*, not just *write*.
4. Note that *clarity* and *effective* communication are mentioned. Being specific and thorough gives you points.
5. This blank space is all-important—we'll teach you how to use it.
6. Use all the space you have; don't rush your writing, as that will make your handwriting harder to read. You may print if you like.
7. Up to you.
8. They're trained to ignore handwriting, but your essay must be legible.
9. Second mention of this space...hint, hint!

10. The only way to get a zero is to write on another topic. So, don't even think of preparing an essay beforehand.

11. Essay prompt: general instructions to think carefully followed by one or two quotes or statements. Note that the theme is very broad.

12. Assignment: the specific question you need to answer is stated here. You are told for the third time to *plan*, and then write, an essay. You're also told to develop a point of view. This type of persuasive writing is the main goal of the essay. Finally, note that you are told to support your position, and that you may use any reasons or examples (i.e., evidence) from your ENTIRE LIFE.

13. Here's that all-important planning space.

OK, now you know what the essay looks like. We've also given you a few hints about the Student Response Sheet, which we'll flesh out in the sections that follow.

(We'll be using this essay prompt throughout the book, so stay tuned.)

WHAT SKILLS DOES THE ESSAY TEST?

The folks at The College Board and the people they hire as readers are not unfair, and they're not sadists. They know you're most likely 16 or 17 years old. They know their test causes a lot of hand-wringing. And they know you have 25 minutes to write an essay on a topic you've never seen before. Here's what they expect:

A first draft

That's it. They don't expect highly polished, finished writing. That would be impossible to produce in 25 minutes. They just want a first draft. Think of an SAT essay as an answer you'd give to an in-class final exam in your English class, rather than a term paper you've worked on for weeks on end. As you'll see, the essay is *easier* than a final exam essay, because you're not expected to demonstrate a semester's worth of knowledge. More on this later.

While The College Board doesn't give you a neat little list of what your essay should include, we do know how the essay will be graded. With that knowledge in hand, we can tell you that your essay should feature the following six qualities:

- Precise use of language
- Clarity of expression

- Sustained focus
- Logical and coherent presentation of ideas
- Ample development of a point of view
- Use of clear reasoning and appropriate evidence

Let's define each of these qualities in a little more detail. We'll spend most of the rest of the book giving you the essential concepts and strategies you'll need to achieve these six broad goals. For now, let's make sure you know what is expected of you.

Precise Use of Language

Precision means being accurate and exact. We're talking about your old friends here: grammar and usage.

Grammar. Know and follow the rules. For example, don't shift your pronouns:

Incorrect: One knows that you can't avoid grammar on the SAT Writing section.

Correct: You know you can't avoid grammar on the SAT Writing section.

Correct: One knows one can't avoid grammar on the SAT Writing section.

Usage. Use words properly. For example, don't write *adverse* (which refers to being opposed to a *situation*) when you mean *averse* (which refers to being opposed to an attitude).

Don't panic if all this grammar and usage talk is confusing. The Essential Concepts section that follows is a focused review and explanation of the relevant grammatical and usage topics you'll need to do well on the essay.

Furthermore—and repeat this mantra to yourself nightly into a mirror—**you can make a few minor usage and grammar errors and still get the highest possible score!**

Clarity of Expression

This is partly a function of following the rules of language (i.e., grammar and usage). However, and more important, clarity of expression is about clear *thought.*

Think of it this way: writing is like sending a radio transmission. Your brain is the transmitter. Your thoughts are the signal. The person reading your essay is the receiver. There are only three ways your signal can be garbled.

1. The signal is garbled inside you, the transmitter. You transmit fine, but the signal is mush. In other words, you understand the rules of language, but you can't seem to produce a coherent argument.
2. The signal is strong but gets garbled in transmission. In other words, you know what you want to say, but you have trouble using the rules of language to say it.
3. The signal is mush and it also gets garbled in transmission. You have problems both in organizing your thoughts and in using the rules of language.

Again, don't worry. Our essential concepts and strategies will alleviate all of these problems. You've come to the right place!

Sustained Focus

You only have 25 minutes to formulate, plan, write, and edit a decent first draft of a persuasive essay. You have no time or space to wander off on tangents; you must devote all your precious time and space to the task at hand. Don't get cute in your writing: "cute" entails taking unnecessary risks.

When you think "SAT essay," think of a well-organized nightly news segment, not a convoluted soap opera plot.

Logical and Coherent Presentation of Ideas

Your essay needs to flow. You need to take a position that is supported by reasons and reinforced by examples. Each sentence should follow naturally from the last, and each paragraph should build on or add to the previous one.

We'll provide you with a process that will allow you to write excellent first-draft essays that flow logically and coherently.

Ample Development of a Point of View

You can't simply state a position without backing it up. *Ample development* means bringing together several lines of evidence. The more types of evidence you bring to bear from various parts of life, the stronger and more persuasive your essay will be.

You'll see how all this works as we go through a practice essay in slow motion.

Use of Clear Reasoning and Appropriate Evidence

It is crucial that you back up your argument with appropriate evidence, which can be defined as *anything you've read, experienced, observed, or heard about.*

The take-home message here is that *all* types of relevant evidence and examples are equally valuable in the eyes of the readers. You may have heard that you must provide hoity-toity literary examples to get a high score. To use a hoity-toity word, that is simply *tosh* (that is to say, "total nonsense").

How unfair would this test be if only those of you who happened to have read and memorized highbrow literature or esoteric scientific theory could get a high score? Remember, the essay is an assessment of how well you use written language to create an argument:

What you say doesn't matter nearly as much as *how well you say it* and *how well you organize it.*

Using a quote from Shakespeare or a reference to quantum physics inappropriately, or in a way that doesn't further the argument or support a point, will not help your essay; in fact, it will hurt it. However, using an appropriate anecdote from your daily life will help, not hurt. It's not the status of the evidence you use that matters—it's the relevance of that piece of evidence to the overall flow and structure of your argument.

WHO CREATES THE ESSAY PROMPTS?

A cackling cabal of chain-smoking, middle-aged failed writers who have long marinated in the bile of their own bitterness get together to make your innocent lives a living hell.

Well, not really. The essay prompts are actually written by a combination of experienced English teachers, writing experts, and college professors, as well as psychometricians, who work together for a long, long time to create prompts that have the following characteristics. According to The College Board's criteria, essay prompts must:

- Allow for an extremely wide variety of possible responses.
- Be clear enough to enable a reasonably well-developed response in 25 minutes.
- Be accessible to *everyone* who takes the SAT, including nonnative speakers.

- Be free of all jargon and specific technical, scientific, cultural, and literary references.
- Not be related to a narrow or specific topic, but rather must be relevant to a wide range of areas of knowledge and activities.
- Not draw on any specific course material or specialized knowledge.

The idea is to provide a prompt that allows millions of test-takers to produce a structured response without providing any unfair advantage to anyone. That's why the prompts sometimes seem bland.

These criteria reinforce the point made earlier about what evidence, reasons, and examples are fair game. Think about it: if you want to create a fair assessment of students' writing ability, you'd want to factor out any advantage that knowing a particular fact, theory, or other piece of knowledge would provide. You'd want to train your readers to ignore the content and concentrate on the one feature of writing that can evaluated objectively: how well a student uses language to structure and support an argument.

In a sense, the SAT Essay is really the twenty-first-century version of the old writing assignment, "What I Did on My Summer Vacation." Old-school teachers really couldn't have cared less what you actually did; they simply wanted to see how well you could come up with a coherent piece of writing, regardless of whether you claimed to have built a dog-house, hitchhiked to Alaska, or been abducted by aliens.

WHO SCORES THE ESSAY?

The cackling cabal? No, simply human beings like you and me, with one crucial difference: they have a lot of experience in teaching and evaluating writing, and they have gone through a lot of specific training.

In order to become an essay-reader you must go through an online training course. Along with an explanation of the scoring rubric (the standards by which your essays will be scored—we'll cover this in the next section) and some technical training in computer and Web technology, prospective readers train with prescored "anchor papers" and are required to pass a qualification test.

It may give you some small satisfaction to know that in order to earn the right to evaluate your essay, your readers themselves have had to pass a tough, high-stakes test. This test requires prospective readers to grade around 40 essays that experts at The College Board have already scored. The prospective readers do not know what these scores are. If the readers do not score at least 70 percent of these essays exactly as the experts at The College Board did, they're dismissed.

HOW IS THE ESSAY SCORED?

Ah, the million-dollar question. Let's talk about a few different aspects of scoring.

Holistic Scoring

Writing—even writing a first draft in 25 minutes—is an extremely complex task. Each element of good writing depends at least partially on every other element. Therefore, essays are graded *holistically*. Holistic scoring means that the parts make up the whole. In other words, the parts that make up an essay, such as grammar, logic, usage, sentence structure, and the use of evidence, cannot be judged in isolation from one another. They can only be understood (and judged) in relation to one another and as parts of a whole essay.

The College Board aims to reward you for what you do *right* rather than punish you for what you do *wrong*.

The Scoring Rubric

The scoring rubric is a chart that instructs readers on how to score the essay. Each of your two readers will give your essay a score between 1 and 6, with 6 being the highest. (If you write nothing, or write on a topic not asked about in the prompt, you'll get a 0.)

The scoring rubric is organized by score level. The several features of a 6 are listed, then the features of a 5, a 4, and so forth.

Dissecting the Scoring Rubric

We're going to look at the scoring rubric in the following way. First, we want to show which features appear across the score levels. That will highlight exactly what the readers are trained to consider when assessing your essay. Then we'll discuss the scoring rubric in detail, feature by feature, showing the differences between and among the various score levels. By studying the scoring rubric in detail, you'll start to understand what your writing should include and what you should avoid. Most important, you'll gain an understanding of how The College Board defines good writing, which is not necessarily identical to how you, your friends, or your parents may define it.

In a sense, we are giving you a crash course in how to grade an SAT essay. In becoming an essay-reader, you will know how to give the real readers exactly what they want.

Here's a distilled version of the scoring rubric, showing what features of writing readers are trained to assess. Note that the first feature is all about holistic scoring—the general overall impression the reader has of your essay.

Score	6	5	4
Features	General overall impression		
	Point of view; critical thinking; examples, reasons, and evidence		
	Organization, focus, coherence, and flow		
	Vocabulary and use of language		
	Sentence structure		
	Errors in grammar and usage		

Score	3	2	1
Features	General overall impression		
	Point of view; critical thinking; examples, reasons, and evidence		
	Organization, focus, coherence, and flow		
	Vocabulary and use of language		
	Sentence structure		
	Errors in grammar and usage		

Note how we divide the upper-half scores (4, 5, and 6) and the lower-half scores (1, 2, and 3). We'll return to the significance of this division in a subsequent section.

This scoring rubric determines which concepts are essential for you to master.

General Overall Impression

Remember, essays are graded holistically; this feature represents an overall impression.

Score Level	Defining Characteristics
6	An **exceptional** essay that shows sustained expertise, but which contains a few minor errors
5	A **successful** essay that shows mostly sustained expertise, even though it contains occasional mistakes or slips in quality
4	An **adequate** essay that shows competence, but which contains more than occasional mistakes or slips in quality
3	An **insufficient** essay that shows signs of evolving competence and features one or more specific flaws
2	A **weak** essay that shows serious limitations, insufficient facility, and which features one or more specific flaws
1	An essentially **deficient** essay that displays fundamental inability and features severe manifestations of one or more specific flaws
0	No essay written. Essay that doesn't respond to the assignment. An illegible essay

These are the general characteristics that readers keep in mind. Let's now discuss the *one or more specific flaws* mentioned in the chart above. These are the more specific features of writing the readers will be on the lookout for.

Point of View; Critical Thinking; and Examples, Reasons, and Evidence

First, let's define some terms:

Point of View: Keep in mind that we're dealing with persuasive writing. You must take a stand on the issue presented, and you'll need to present a definite point of view.

Critical Thinking: Your essay will be graded, in part, on how deep your analysis is and how unique your thoughts are.

Examples, Reasons, and Evidence: We've touched on this before. All of your experience and knowledge is fair game—the key is to use *appropri-*

ate examples that help build your case. You should have at least a couple of reasons for your point of view and ample evidence, including examples, to back up your reasons. (We'll provide a template for you in Essential Strategies that will ensure that your essay fulfills these requirements.)

Now let's look at the different score levels with these features in mind:

Score Level	Defining Characteristics
6	Impressively insightful point of view Outstanding critical thinking Completely appropriate reasons, examples, and evidence to support point of view
5	Well-developed point of view Strong critical thinking Generally appropriate reasons, examples, and evidence to support point of view
4	Fairly well developed point of view Adequate critical thinking Mostly appropriate reasons, examples, and evidence to support point of view
3	Develops a point of view Some evidence of critical thinking, but inconsistently apparent Sometimes inappropriate reasons, examples, and evidence to support point of view
2	Develops a vague point of view Little evidence of critical thinking Insufficient or inappropriate reasons, examples, and evidence to support point of view
1	Does not develop a point of view No evidence of critical thinking Little or no evidence to support point of view

The scoring rubric has a lot to say on these three components of good writing. That should tell you something: the SAT wants you to demonstrate the ability to create a reasonable argument that displays some independent and reasonably deep thinking that you *support* rather than simply *state*.

Critical thinking is all about building a good argument; encouraging and rewarding critical thinking is the goal of the essay. (We'll discuss the basics of argumentation in a subsequent section.)

Organization, Focus, Coherence, and Flow

A primary characteristic of good writing is a well-organized and coherent argument that is **focused** and flows naturally. Here is how these features play out in the scoring rubric:

Score Level	Defining Characteristics
6	Well organized Tightly focused Tight coherence Smooth flow of ideas
5	Well organized Focused Coheres reasonably well Mostly smooth flow of ideas
4	Generally organized Generally focused Shows some coherence Discernable but not particularly smooth flow of ideas
3	Partially organized Partially unfocused Some incoherent portions Interrupted or disrupted flow of ideas
2	Poorly organized Mostly unfocused Systemic problems with incoherence Flow of ideas difficult to discern
1	Disorganized Unfocused Incoherent Flow of ideas impossible to discern or entirely absent

Compare this chart to the others in this section. Note that the SAT is pretty tough on disorganization, lack of focus, and incoherence. In fact, we can probably conclude that this feature of writing is the biggest concern. Readers want to see how well you can create, plan, and execute a persuasive piece of writing. If you're disorganized or unfocused, you'll be unpersuasive.

Don't worry—we have a plan and a method for you. You'll encounter it soon. But let's continue dissecting the scoring rubric.

Vocabulary and Use of Language

One component of effective writing is choosing the appropriate word and using a varied vocabulary. Study the following chart, noting the differences between the characteristics that define each score level:

Score Level	Defining Characteristics
6	Skilled use of language Varied, accurate, and appropriate vocabulary
5	Capable use of language Appropriate vocabulary
4	Satisfactory but inconsistent use of language Generally appropriate vocabulary
3	Inconsistent use of language that shows signs of evolving competence Some inappropriate word choice; weak vocabulary
2	Insufficient use of language Very limited vocabulary or incorrect word choice
1	Basic vocabulary errors

The take-home message here is that misusing highfalutin, ten-dollar words will definitely hurt you. Using appropriate, reasonably varied vocabulary will help get you toward the top of the scoring rubric.

Sentence Structure

Bill went to the store. Bill got some milk. Bill met Jane. Jane got some gum. Bill and Jane said good-bye. Bill went home.

Are you bored yet? The SAT will look for varied sentence structure. Simply writing "subject-verb-object" declarative sentences over and over again will put a ceiling on your score. Let's see what the scoring rubric looks for at each score level.

Score Level	Defining Characteristics
6	Displays meaningful variety
5	Displays variety
4	Displays some variety
3	Does not display variety Displays problems
2	Displays frequent problems
1	Displays serious and widespread problems

Merely displaying some variety in your sentences will help get you a 4, 5, or 6. But note the difference between a 5 and a 6: the purposeful and significant use of particular types of sentences will earn you a 6. (We'll discuss the basics of sentence structure in Essential Concepts.)

Errors in Grammar, Usage, and Mechanics

Grammar, usage, and mechanics are the rules of written language. But note how forgiving the SAT is about these rules. While you can't ignore them, you do have some grammatical leeway: the readers are realistic about what degree of accuracy is reasonable to expect in a 25-minute, high-pressure essay.

Score Level	Defining Characteristics
6	Free of most errors
5	On the whole, free of most errors
4	Has some errors
3	Has a lot of errors
2	Has so many errors that meaning is partially hidden
1	Persistent and widespread errors that obscure meaning

Note that even a 6 does not need to be error-free. Readers know that this is a *first draft* written by teenagers under strict time constraints and a lot of pressure. Readers are out to give you the highest score they can. The next section will show you exactly how.

How the Essay-Readers Apply the Scoring Rubric

Remember, the overarching principle of essay-scoring is to do so holistically. So, while readers use the scoring rubric as a guide, they also adhere to several other general principles and procedures when scoring your essay.

First, remember that your essay will be read not by one, but by two different readers. If their scores differ by more than one point, a third, very experienced reader is brought in. Second, readers are trained to read your entire essay quickly to get a general impression. They then score it immediately. That is a very effective way to keep the readers focused on holistic grading: readers don't have the time to get nitpicky. Scoring decisions often occur in two steps:

- Step 1: Readers first decide whether an essay is in the top or bottom half of the scoring rubric—is it a 1, 2, 3 or a 4, 5, 6?
- Step 2: Then they make decisions within the "half"—is it a 4 or a 5? Is it maybe a 6?

Third, The College Board demands that readers read "supportively." That means readers are trained to look for positive aspects to reward rather than negative aspects to punish. That means that **the readers are literally rooting for you**.

Fourth, readers are trained to ignore handwriting as much as is humanly possible. Particularly difficult handwriting will be bumped up to more experienced readers. However, one way to get a zero is to write illegibly. So, while we don't recommend totally retooling your handwriting, make sure to be as neat as you can.

Fifth, despite what you may have heard, a longer essay doesn't equal a higher score. Longer is not necessarily better. In fact, readers are specifically told to judge essays as is, holistically, and by using the scoring rubric. If a shorter essay earns a 6, so be it. Furthermore, and most important, the idea that writing a long essay will automatically raise your score leads to some of the worst possible essay-writing strategies. The SAT wants to see a first draft that develops a well-thought-out and well-supported point of view on the issue that is written engagingly, with varied and mostly correct language. The point is to achieve that goal, not to attain some "magic" length within the allotted time.

Finally, the readers couldn't care less whether you quote Plato's *Republic*, your own diary, or an advertising jingle. What matters is the *appropriateness* of your evidence, examples, and reasons, not the status of the knowledge you use to support your argument and point of view.

THE BIGGER PICTURE

Your essay score is factored into your multiple-choice Writing score. You will receive a multiple-choice Writing scaled subscore between 20 and 80. You will receive an essay subscore between 2 and 12. (Remember, you get *two* readers, each grading you on a scale from 1 to 6.)

So what do the essay subscores actually mean? The College Board recommends treating them similarly to the more familiar 200–800 scaled scores of the other sections. A 560 in Math, Critical Reading, or Writing is not really a 560. It's the middle of a range (usually ten or twelve or so points in either direction). So when a school sees a 560 in Critical Reading, they're supposed to think something like this: "Well, on any given Saturday, this kid could have gotten anywhere from, say, a 540 to a 580. He's a *mid-500-er.*"

Likewise, if you get a 3 on your essay, The College Board recommends, and schools have been told, that your ability is anywhere from a "low 3" to a "high 3." Additionally, even with all the effort The College Board has put into standardizing this writing assessment, they realize that since we're all human, there will be some variation in scoring. It's likely that the distinction between an upper-half (4, 5, 6) and a lower-half essay (1, 2, 3) may be as important to a school as the actual number itself. Note that the scale is even: there is no middle score. That implies that readers must make a distinction between the upper and lower halves of the scoring rubric for the bulk of the essays they read.

The essay subscore counts for about one-third of the final scaled Writing score. The multiple-choice Writing subscore counts for the rest. The SAT has a formula that combines the multiple-choice subscore with the essay subscore. Don't worry about it—no one outside of The College Board really knows what it is, but you can rest assured that it will be applied to everyone fairly. The bottom line is that the essay counts for about one-ninth of your total SAT score. (The essay is a third of the Writing score, and the Writing score is a third of the total, along with Math and Critical Reading.)

The essay only counts for one-ninth of the whole test? What's the big hoo-hah, then? Well, a ninth is still a ninth. And there are some other uses for the essay that you may not have heard of. Colleges and universities have the right and ability to do exactly what SAT readers will do: download a PDF of your essay. They can then use your essay to make placement decisions for freshman writing courses or as a comparison to your admissions essay.

NOW WHAT DO I DO?

You've learned quite a bit about what the essay looks like, what's expected of you, how you will be graded, what those scores mean, and how they will be used.

You may be thinking, "Great! I totally get what the readers expect of me and how I'll be scored. But I need help constructing a persuasive essay. I need advice on how to construct and support an argument; I need to review the basic language skills I'll be judged on. Don't just tell me: *show* me."

No fear: that's exactly what we're going to do for the remainder of this book. Here's the plan:

1. We will review some of the essential concepts you'll need to hone your language skills. We'll also give you an outline to use for your own essay.

2. We'll present the essential strategies and step method you'll use to create an impressive, coherent, well-organized, and well-supported essay.

3. We'll use the essay prompt and assignment you saw at the beginning of the book to work through the entire process together, demonstrating how to deploy all you've learned in slow motion.

4. You'll be ready to practice on your own, using your newly acquired essay-writing and essay-grading skills.

ESSENTIAL CONCEPTS

Your ability to choose, support, and develop an argument will determine much of your essay score. And language is the tool that you'll use to construct and convey your argument.

To help you maximize your essay score, we've collected the most relevant elements of language and writing an argument you'll need to maximize your score. As you study these concepts, don't get too caught up in the formal or grammatical names. The names are there simply because we have to call these concepts *something*, but don't be intimidated or turned off! Concentrate on the *concepts* behind the names.

To make these concepts more digestible, we've pared down the huge subject of writing to what actually matters most for the essay. We've also taken some small liberties with terminology for the sake of simplicity.

CREATING A STRONG WRITTEN ARGUMENT

You've seen several key terms in the essay prompt and assignment, as well as in the scoring rubric. Here they are: *reasons, examples, appropriate evidence, organization, support, point of view, position, focus, coherence, development, flow.*

These are all features of a strong written argument. A strong argument has a recognizable structure—especially for a timed essay like the SAT's. The following chart presents this structure and relates it to these key terms that the SAT clearly emphasizes. Some of the correspondences are obvious; others aren't. **This is the structure you should follow for your SAT essay:**

Essay Structure		What It Means
Thesis Statement		This is a one-sentence statement of your point of view. It's the position on the issue that you'll defend and support.
Reason I	Example 1	Each reason should support your thesis statement. Examples are evidence. Each example should appropriately support its reason.
Reason I	Example 2	
Reason I	Example 3	
Reason II	Example 4	
Reason II	Example 5	
Reason II	Example 6	
Reason III	Example 7	
Reason III	Example 8	
Reason III	Example 9	
Conclusion		Recaps your thesis statement and applies your position more broadly.

Looks a lot like an outline, doesn't it? Very perceptive of you—we'll return to that in Essential Strategies. For now, let's define and flesh out some terms not on the chart.

- **Organization.** Your essay needs to be organized; using the essay structure above will give you this organization.
- **Focus.** Note that there is a hierarchical structure to writing an essay. The thesis is supported by three reasons; each reason is supported by three examples. The conclusion restates the thesis. There is no room for wandering.
- **Coherence.** In a coherent essay, all the parts relate to one another clearly and naturally. This, too, flows naturally from the essay structure described above.
- **Development.** In terms of writing, *development* means stating a point of view and then supporting it with well-chosen reasons and evidence or examples. A good essay takes the reader by the hand and walks him or her along the path of the writer's argument without allowing the reader to stumble.

- **Flow.** Well-written essays need to *go* somewhere. The reasons should follow in a logical and natural way. Most writing has a beginning, a middle, and an end. Your essay should as well: that's the primary way to determine flow.

We've built this argument structure into our step method, as you'll see in Essential Strategies. Everything about it grows naturally out of the essay prompt and scoring rubric. The essay is primarily concerned with the *structure* of your writing. If you construct and support a clear and strong argument, you will be well on your way to a high score.

BASICS OF LANGUAGE

As you saw in our close study of the scoring rubric, sophisticated use of language will raise your score.

Your essay score will primarily be based on the quality of your critical thinking and your ability to present a strong argument. But without some basic language skills, you won't be able to convey your thinking or argument. Your writing should be a clear window that readers can look through to see your argument. What follows are some key elements of language chosen not so much to prevent mistakes but rather to give you as many options for communicating your meaning as effectively, clearly, and engagingly as you can.

We've broken the basics of language into five main sections. Each section relates to a specific feature of the scoring rubric. Here's a handy chart:

Feature of Language	Feature of the Scoring Rubric
Verbs	Sentence structure, coherence, flow, grammar, and usage
Agreement	Coherence, flow, grammar, and usage
Modifiers and modification	Coherence, flow, sentence structure, grammar, and usage
Clause organization	Organization, coherence, flow, sentence structure, grammar, and usage
Usage	Vocabulary, grammar, and usage

Verbs

Good writing depends on actions and chronology—who did what to whom when? If you want to prevent your readers from getting lost, make sure you drive them in the right direction.

Past vs. Present Perfect

The **past** tense signifies that something occurred or existed in the past. It is indicated by an *–ed* at the end of a word, or by an equivalent irregular form, such as *flew* or *thought*:

Barbara **worked** in New York long ago.

This means that Barbara worked in New York at some *definite* point in the past. She no longer works there.

The **present perfect** tense refers either to something that began in the past and continues into the present or something that occurred in the past but still has some bearing on the present. It is indicated by using *has/have* plus the *–ed* (or the equivalent irregular) form of a verb:

Barbara **has worked** in New York before.

Unlike the previous sentence, this sentence means that Barbara worked in New York at some *unspecified* point in the past.

Barbara **has worked** in New York for twenty years.

This sentence means that Barbara started working in New York at some point in the past, never stopped, and is still working there in the present.

There are a few words that signal that the present perfect rather than the past should be used. These **signpost words** are:

Signpost Word	Example	Comment
ever	*Bill has read novels ever since he retired.*	Notice how this sentence uses both the present perfect and the past. *Bill has read novels* means that Bill started reading novels at some point in the past and still reads them in the present. *[E]ver since he retired* means that Bill started reading novels at a definite point in the past—when *he retired.*
never	*Evan has never been one to restrain himself.*	This means that at no point in the past—and up to the present moment—has Evan been able to control himself. A state of being that began at some indefinite point in the past has continued up to the present moment.
since	*Since learning to swim, Ingmar has enjoyed the ocean.*	Again, an action has occurred at some indefinite point in the past and continues to this day.
yet	*The book hasn't been written yet.*	A particular state of being—that of not completing the book—has not occurred since some indefinite point in the past and continues not to occur up to the present moment.

Past vs. Past Perfect

The **past perfect** tense (also known as "pluperfect") refers to something that began and ended *before* something else occurred in the past. The past perfect tense is "more past than the past." It is indicated by using *had* plus the *–ed* (or equivalent irregular) form:

Darwin **had visited** the Cape de Verde Islands before he visited the Galapagos Islands.

This means that Darwin's presence in the Cape de Verde Islands *preceded* his presence in the Galapagos Islands, which *itself* occurred in the past.

As a rule, if you have two actions that occurred in the past, put the one that occurred deeper in the past in the past perfect tense. The more recent action should be in the past tense.

If-clauses

What's the difference between the following two sentences?

If I really study this book, I will raise my essay score.
If I were the president, I would do things a lot differently.

The first sentence states that if a condition is fulfilled (really studying this book), then a particular action will result (raising your essay score). The second sentence states something that's contrary to fact, something imagined that exists only in thought. The person making that statement is *not* the president, clearly, but is projecting himself into that person's situation.

The first sentence is in the **indicative** mood; the second sentence is in the **subjunctive** mood. (Again, don't worry too much about the names used here.)

The main point is the form of the second (subjunctive) sentence. The *if* clause should never include a *would* verb; *would* is used only in the second clause, which we'll call the *would* clause:

Incorrect	Correct	Comment on Correct Version
If you would have stayed longer, you would have had more fun.	If you had stayed longer, you would have had more fun.	*If*-clause is in past perfect *Would*-clause is in present perfect

Active Voice vs. Passive Voice

Voice is a feature of verbs that shows whether the subject of a sentence is doing the action or having the action done to it.

Passive: The citizens were not notified.
Active: The mayor did not notify the citizens.

Note that the **passive voice** allows a writer (or speaker) to dodge responsibility by hiding the identity of the person executing the action. "Gee, the citizens just weren't notified. Oh, well. Such is life." The active version of the sentence names names and ascribes actions to a real, live person.

For that reason, the passive voice is most widely used in politics, the business world, or in any other activity involving a bureaucracy. Educators and stylists have been pushing for wider use of the active voice: the SAT reflects this trend. As you may have heard your English teacher say, *verb* your way through your writing. Use active, focused, forceful verbs, not the same weak passive verbs over and over again.

The **active voice** usually requires far fewer words than the passive voice to convey the same idea:

Passive: The guitar was handed by the roadie to the rock star. (11 words)
Active: The roadie handed the guitar to the rock star. (9 words)
Passive: The investigation of the war crimes alleged to have been committed by the occupying forces was carried out by an international agency. (22 words)
Active: An international agency led the investigation of the occupying forces' alleged war crimes. (13 words)

Notice in both examples how we replaced a form of *to be* with a more active verb:

First example: *was* replaced by *handed*
Second example: *was* replaced by *led*

If your sentence contains a form of *to be,* be on the lookout for an unnecessary passive construction. Concision is the hallmark of good writing; the active voice is far leaner than the bloated passive voice.

Agreement
If words don't agree with one another in a sentence, meaning is obscured. There are several types of agreement.

Subject/Verb Agreement

Life jackets is necessary.
Rain are wet.

It's easy to see what's wrong with these sentences. The subjects of these sentences (*life jackets* and *rain*) do not match their verbs (*is* and *are*, respectively). *Life jackets* are plural, but *is* is singular; *rain* is singular, but *are* is plural. Subjects and verbs must match, or "agree."

Life jackets are necessary.
Rain is wet.

Intervening Clauses and Phrases

The tricky thing for the essay is that you're going to want to vary your sentence structure. However, you need to vary your sentences grammatically, but in such a way that doesn't obscure your meaning. So let's look at some more complex sentences with subject/verb agreement in mind.

The prescription of antidepressants, which is driven by the fact that medications are more likely to be covered by insurance than psychotherapy, often lead to burying the sources of depression.

See the error? If not, get rid of the intervening clause:

The prescription of antidepressants often lead to burying the sources of depression.

Can you see it now? If not, isolate the subject and verb:

The prescriptions of antidepressants often lead to burying the sources
        Subject   Verb
of depression.

Antidepressants is not the subject—the *prescription of antidepressants* is. *Prescription* is singular; *lead* is the plural form of the verb. You need the singular form of the verb to match the singular subject.

The correct version is:

The prescription of antidepressants, which is driven by that fact that medications are more likely to be covered by insurance than psychotherapy, often leads to burying the sources of depression.

Hidden and Compound Subjects

Here's another typical error you may commit when you try to vary your sentence structure:

Inside the tank is a goldfish and a snail.

Tricky! The subject is hidden here—it's **not** *the tank*. What if you flip the sentence around so that the subject, which we're accustomed to seeing at the beginning of a sentence, comes first?

A goldfish and a snail is inside the tank.

The *is* sticks out more when the sentence is rewritten this way; it should be *are*. *A goldfish and a snail* is a compound subject; compound subjects take plural verbs. Only the word *and* can create a compound subject. *As well as, or,* and *along with* do **not** create compound subjects:

Rock and jazz **are** influential musical styles.
Rock, as well as jazz, **is** an influential musical style.
Rock, along with jazz, **is** an influential musical style.
Rock or jazz **is** an influential musical style.

Singular or Plural?

What's wrong with the following sentence?

Neither of those two musical styles are as influential as blues.

The problem is that *neither, either,* and *none* take singular, not plural, verbs. The correction is:

Neither of those two musical styles is as influential as blues.

Finally, watch out for nouns that seem plural but are actually singular, such as:

The **series** of plays was very entertaining.
The **team** was crushed by the loss.
The **couple** finds life together to be challenging.

Series, team, and *couple* are singular nouns that refer to groups. *Group,* actually, is another good example. By definition, a group has more than one member, but a group itself is singular: one group; many groups.

Noun/Number Agreement

All people enjoy maintaining their yard.

You might think this sentence is OK, but it's incorrect. As written, it means that every single person currently alive, as well as all persons that have ever lived, enjoy maintaining the **one yard** they've all shared! That's a big yard.

Nouns have to agree in number—start with plural, end with plural; start with singular, end with singular. This sentence should be:

All **people** enjoy maintaining their **yards**.

Here's another common mistake to avoid:

Bob, Jim, and Neil are planning to give up music in order to become a writer.

How can **three** people, *Bob, Jim, and Neil,* become **one** *writer?* Well, they can't:

Bob, Jim, and Neil are planning to give up music in order to become **writers**.

Countability

Another common error involving nouns is what we call **countability**. Look at the following sentences:

I have many disappointments.
You would be wise to show less hatred toward others.

Both sentences are correct. *Disappointments* are something one could count; *disappointments* are discrete entities like puppies or galaxies or staplers. *Hatred,* however, cannot be counted; *hatred* is an abstract state of being, as are *oppression, liberty,* and *apathy.* Concrete entities—*air* and *water,* to name two—can be noncountable as well. (*Putting on airs* and *parting the waters* are figuratively countable uses of these non-countable nouns.)

Countability is most often indicated via the *less/fewer* and *number/amount* pairings. Here's a handy chart:

Noun	Countable?	Use	Example
happiness	No	less	Why aim for less happiness than you can achieve?
virus	Yes	fewer	There are fewer viruses than bacteria.
fear	No	less	The less fear we feel, the better we are able to think.
joke	Yes	fewer	If you told fewer jokes, the class could make more progress.
computer	Yes	number	The number of home computers has skyrocketed in the past twenty years.
courage	No	amount	The amount of courage a leader inspires is a telling measure of his value.
flower	Yes	number	I have a number of flowers on my kitchen table.
joy	No	amount	The value of one's life is proportional to the amount of joy in it.

Pronoun/Number Agreement

Did everyone forget to bring their raincoat with them?

The question above is grammatically incorrect.

Everyone is singular, strange as that may seem. You might think that everyone refers to a collection of people, but it refers to each individual in a collection of people—every*one*.

To highlight this error, substitute the equivalent phrase *each of you* into the sentence:

Did each of you forget to bring their raincoat with them?

The pronoun *their* is plural, but it refers back to a singular subject, *each of you*—or, in the previous sentence, *everyone*. The proper form is:

Did everyone forget to bring his or her raincoat with him or her?

Yes, this is cumbersome, but correct.

The following words behave just like *everyone: anyone, no one, nobody, every, each.*

Check out this sentence:

Spacely Sprockets reported today that their workforce had accepted management's demands.

Sprockets may be plural, but presumably there is only one company called *Spacely Sprockets.* If it's a single company, it requires a singular pronoun:

Spacely Sprockets reported today that **its** workforce had accepted management's demands.

Pronoun Shift

Watch out for **pronoun shift** too:

Incorrect: If **you** start with a particular pronoun, **one** shouldn't shift to another later on in the sentence.

Correct: If **one** would like to do as well as **one** can on the essay, **one** should keep this common error in mind.

Correct: That way, **you** will be happy with the score **you** receive.

Ambiguous and Vague Pronouns

Ambiguous pronouns lack a clear antecedent; vague pronouns lack an antecedent altogether. **Antecedent** refers to the noun (or pronoun) that a pronoun refers to (*ante* meaning "before" in Latin).

In the following sentence, the pronoun is bolded:

Donna told Marie about **her** knitting.

Whose knitting are we talking about, Donna's or Marie's? They're both women, so it's impossible to tell. Replace *her* with either *Donna's* or *Marie's* and you've solved the problem:

Donna told Marie about **Donna's** knitting.

or

Donna told Marie about **Marie's** knitting.

Be on the lookout for all kinds of ambiguities. Look at the following sentence:

Mike gave his brother a bass amplifier that he used every chance he could get.

This seems less ambiguous because we tend to interpret the sentence according to our experience and expectations: "Mike's a nice guy; he gave his brother a bass amp. That brother used that amp every chance he could get. How touching!"

That's all well and good, except that it is possible that Mike gave his brother a bass amp and that Mike, not his brother, used it every chance he got. Maybe Mike's a selfish brother. Maybe Mike's brother hated the amp. The point is, we've got an ambiguous pronoun (*he*), and that obscures meaning.

Now, what's wrong with the following sentence?

They say that global warming will only get worse.

On its own, the *they* in this sentence has no antecedent at all. There are many ways to rewrite this sentence; here's one option:

A panel of expert climatologists says that global warming will only get worse.

Now you have a clear statement. Note, however, that if the original sentence had been embedded in a paragraph, it would be clear who *they* refers to:

The world's scientific experts agree. They say that global warming will only get worse.

Context is everything; in this context, *they* has a clear antecedent: *the world's scientific experts.*

Modifiers and Modification

Modifying Words

A **modifier** is a word or a phrase that describes another word or phrase. The most familiar examples are **adjectives** and **adverbs**. Adjectives describe nouns or pronouns; adverbs describe verbs, adjectives, or other adverbs.

Here are some examples:

Adjectives
The **loud** noise shocked us.
The **fruitful** hypothesis led to interesting experiments.

Adverbs
Al spoke **convincingly**.
Stephen fought **viciously**.

A common error is using an adjective when an adverb is required. For example, why is the following sentence incorrect?

I take that remark serious.

Serious is an adjective modifying *take,* which is a verb. That's a no-no; it should be:

I take that remark **seriously**.

You should also strive to use the proper form of an adjective. Adjectives can take three forms, as you can see in the following chart:

Descriptive	Comparative	Superlative
hot	hotter	hottest
dull	duller	dullest
complex	more complex	most complex
good	better	best
bad	worse	worst

Most adjectives follow the forms exemplified by *hot* and *dull.* Some, like *complex,* require *more* for the **comparative** and *most* for the **superlative**. *Good* and *bad,* and some others, are irregular.

Consider the following sentences.

Of the three cars, that one is cheaper.
That car is cheapest than this one.

Both are incorrect. The comparative form should be used with two objects; the superlative with three or more objects. The sentences should be:

Of the three cars, that one is **cheapest**.
That car is **cheaper** than this one.

Modifying Phrases

Phrases can act as modifiers too, and this is where things get a little trickier. Mastering this concept will greatly improve your essay.

Roaring into the Florida sky, the space shuttle awed the spectators.

The phrase *roaring into the Florida sky* is a unit that modifies *the space shuttle*. But what if we wrote the sentence as follows?

Roaring into the Florida sky, the spectators were awed by the space shuttle.

What this second sentence is saying is that *the spectators* were *roaring into the Florida sky.* That would truly be an awe-inspiring sight!

This is the storied **dangling modifier**. The modifier *roaring into the Florida sky* dangles off the front of the sentence, unconnected to *the space shuttle*, the phrase it modifies.

Some other examples of dangling modifiers follow; they can be pretty funny once you recognize the error:

Incorrect: Smoking a big cigar, the baby was admired by its father.
Comment: There's very little chance that any baby would be precocious enough to smoke a cigar.
Correct: Smoking a big cigar, the father admired his baby.
Incorrect: Playing drums for too long, there is a chance of injury.

Comment: This modifier is dangling by a thread—what could *playing drums for too long* modify in this sentence?

Correct: If you play drums for too long, you risk injury.

Incorrect: Swearing in frustration, my computer continually crashed as I rushed to complete my paper.

Comment: Was *the computer* doing the *swearing*? I don't think technology is quite there yet!

Correct: Swearing in frustration, I rushed to complete my paper as my computer crashed continually.

Incorrect: To get a high score on the essay, a lot of material needs to be mastered.

Comment: We're missing the noun that needs modification—who needs to master a lot of material?

Correct: To get a high score on the essay, test-takers need to master a lot of material.

Another frequent writing error that obscures meaning is the **misplaced modifier**. Here's an example:

> The teacher posted the grades for the students earned on the midterm.

In this sentence, the phrase *earned on the midterm* seems to modify *the students*, when it should modify *the grades*. This is confusing; here's a rewrite:

> The teacher posted the grades earned on the midterm for the students.

Clause Organization

A **clause** is a group of words that has a subject and a predicate. Sentences can have one clause or many clauses. Clauses are the building blocks of sentences and are very important units of meaning; essentially, they create a logical flow. How clauses and phrases are positioned and the punctuation used to connect them generates the flow that all good writing must have. Varying your clause structure will be greatly rewarded on the essay.

The following sentence has three clauses, each of which is underlined:

<u>Einstein shocked most of his peers</u> when <u>he proved that measurements of</u>
Clause 1 Clause 2
<u>time, length, and mass were relative to the observer</u> because <u>Newtonian</u>
Clause 2 Clause 3
<u>physics had assumed these measurements to be absolute regardless of the observer.</u>
Clause 3

The words that are not underlined are the all-important connections between the clauses. They guide the reader from clause to clause, and essay-readers will reward your ability to choose these words appropriately. Appropriate connections require that you follow logic as well as grammar. As much as any feature of language, their proper use creates the flow so valued by the essay-readers.

In the sentence above, *when* lets the reader know that what shocked most of Einstein's peers is about to be announced. Furthermore, since *when* is a temporal word, you know that something specific happened at some specific point in time. *Because* lets you know that the reason why his peers were so stunned is about to be revealed.

Logical flow is most obviously transmitted by signpost words, which often link paragraphs. English has many such guide words and phrases. Here's a handy list of some common ones; be sure you can use them properly:

and	even	so
also	for	still
although	however	thus
as well as	moreover	therefore
because	nevertheless	though
but	no less than	yet
consequently	or	
despite	otherwise	

The Weak *And*

One common feature of poor clause connection is "the weak *and*." Think about it: what does *and* mean? It's pretty much the word version of the + symbol. *And* denotes addition or the mere presence of two equivalent things at the same time or in the same place:

Frank likes beans and Mongo likes cheese.

+ symbol. *And* denotes addition or the mere presence of two equivalent things at the same time or in the same place:

Frank likes beans and Mongo likes cheese.

You feel like shrugging your shoulders and saying, "Well, Frank likes his beans; Mongo likes his cheese. To each his own, I guess." *And* doesn't *lead* the reader anywhere. It makes no causal connection. It stops the flow dead in its tracks.

The following sentence has the same problem:

Darwin's theory of natural selection shocked Victorian England and a pillar of Victorian culture had been that a benevolent deity had specially created all species.

Huh? You know that this sentence just cries out for causation; substitute *because* for *and* to make this sentence flow:

Darwin's theory of natural selection shocked Victorian England **because** a pillar of Victorian culture had been that a benevolent deity had specially created all species.

Commas, Semicolons, and Colons

A related and much-misunderstood concept is the use of **commas, semicolons**, and **colons**. These punctuation marks act as connection words: they're shorthand for certain types of connections between clauses. They're critical both for logical flow and for sentence structure variety.

If a period is a "full stop," and a comma is a "pause," then a semicolon is somewhere in between, but closer to a full stop. Use it to separate two clauses that could stand alone as sentences:

All music gives me some amount of joy; some types of music give me more joy than others.

All music gives me some amount of joy. Some types of music give me more joy than others.

Use a colon either to "announce" a list or to magnify or exemplify what preceded the colon:

> You'll need a few key items on test day: a number-two pencil, a calculator, and a sweater.

> Most of the troublemakers in my class are actually gifted students: Kim, for example, consistently receives high scores on aptitude tests.

> Often what we consider "traditional" cuisine is really a recent invention: until Columbus, for example, Italian food lacked tomatoes.

Like semicolons, colons can separate clauses that can stand alone. However, if you use a colon, you'll be stressing that the clause after the colon follows sequentially from the phrase that precedes the colon:

> All music gives me some amount of joy; some types of music give me more joy than others.

> All music gives me some amount of joy: some types of music give me more joy than others.

The first sentence indicates that the speaker gets some amount of joy from any type of music, but, as an almost statistical point, that some types of music give him more joy than others. The second sentence places more emphasis on the fact that select types of music give him more joy than others.

Comma Issues

Commas are the hardest of all punctuation marks to master. Don't fret—just concentrate on avoiding the most common error: the misuse of *that* and *which*. When in doubt, use *that*. If you think you must use *which*, use a comma to set off the *which* clause:

> The tree that I like to climb the most is in my best friend's backyard.

> The tree I loved, which the town just cut down, was in Roosevelt Park.

Another common error is the **comma splice**. (These are also known as "fused sentences" and "run-on sentences.") Basically, don't use a comma where a period or semicolon is required, as in the following incorrect sentence:

> The essay is not the place to stretch the rules of grammar, avoid comma splices.

Fix this with a semicolon, colon, or period:

> The essay is not the place to stretch the rules of grammar; avoid comma splices.

or

> The essay is not the place to stretch the rules of grammar: avoid comma splices.

or

> The essay is not the place to stretch the rules of grammar. Avoid comma splices.

Watch out for **sentence fragments**, too. A fragment occurs when a dependent clause, which cannot stand on its own, is forced to do so. These clauses often contain **gerunds** (-*ing* constructions) or **infinitives**:

> Proceeding to the next step.
> To unite the two parties.

Sentences need both a subject and a predicate. Don't use fragments on purpose—again, the essay is not the place to take chances.

Comparisons

In this section, we'll explore two other crucial features of clause structure.

What's wrong with the following sentence?

> Like England, parliaments have been adopted in other countries.

What exactly is being compared here? *England* and *parliaments* or *England* and *other countries*? Right, *England* and *other countries*. This is a perfect example of how imprecise use of language will obscure your meaning and lower your subscore.

To fix this, put the two things being compared next to each other:

Like England, other countries have adopted parliaments.

Also note the passive construction of the first, incorrect sentence. You'll find that these errors compound and entail each other. Luckily, fixing one often leads to fixing others automatically!

Another, trickier, example:

Like classical economics, Darwin focused on individuals.

It doesn't make sense to compare *classical economics* to *Darwin.* You're comparing an area of study to a person. You must always compare like with like. Here are some ways to fix this problem:

Like classical economics, Darwinian evolution focused on individuals.

Like classical economists, Darwin focused on individuals.

As you strive to vary your sentence structure, watch out for the long intervening clause!

Like classical economics, which is still the reigning orthodoxy, Darwin focused on individuals.

It doesn't matter how long the intervening clause is—this is still incorrect. While it's a good idea to vary your sentence length, be on the lookout for agreement and comparison errors.

Like vs. As

Another key concept is the difference between *like* and *as*. Use *like* to compare **nouns** (persons, places, things, or ideas):

That man looks like **Mick Jagger.**

Use *as* to compare **verbs**:

That man **sings** soulfully, just as Mick Jagger **does.**

Parallelism

Parallel structure is not only a sign of good writing, but it also serves to vary your sentence structure, carry your argument forward, and clarify your meaning. It's also easy to grasp and use.

First, certain stock phrases have to follow a certain form. Look at this chart:

Form	Example
neither/nor	That cyclist has neither **the equipment** nor **the endurance** to attempt a 100-mile ride.
either/or	You can have either **a bagel** or **a donut**.
not only/but also	Writing a successful essay requires not only **good argumentation** but also **effective use of language**.
the more/the more	The more **you eat**, the more **weight you'll gain**.
the less/the less	The less **pollution we breathe**, the less **chance we'll have of becoming ill later in life**.
both/and	Both **ants** and **bees** cooperate so closely that they could be considered "superorganisms."
if/then	If **you want a high score on your essay**, then **study this book and practice**.

These forms should always be maintained: don't write *neither/or* or *not only/but*.

Second, learn to apply parallelism properly. Look at this sentence:

I walk a lot, but on the other hand, I seem to spend a lot of time sitting on the couch.

You have the *other hand,* but where's the first hand? This sentence is not parallel. To fix it, write:

On the one hand, I walk a lot, but on the other hand, I seem to spend a lot of time sitting on the couch.

What's wrong with the following sentence?

Not only do I like to swim, but I also like water-skiing.

The verb in the first clause is an infinitive, *to swim*. But the verb in the second part is a gerund, *water-skiing*. Fix it in one of two ways:

Not only do I like to swim, but I also like to water-ski.
Not only do I like swimming, but I also like water-skiing.

The need for parallel structure arises in series as well. The following sentence is incorrect:

Jane likes knitting, boxing, and to read.

Again, you have two ways to fix this:

Jane likes knitting, boxing, and reading.
Jane likes to knit, to box, and to read.

Another kind of parallelism mistake is the following:

Composing with a computer is better than when you compose with pen and paper.

To fix this, make sure your verbs are in the same form:

Composing with a computer is better than composing with pen and paper.

As usual, pay special attention to sentences you write that have long intervening clauses:

Composing with a computer, which allows you to hear what you're composing as you work, is better than when you compose with pen and paper.

Change *when you compose* to *composing*, just as we did in the previous incorrect sentence.

Usage

Word Choice

Word choice is a key feature of the scoring rubric. The proper and appropriate use of words can really impress. Let's start with the much more concrete and discrete concept of proper word choice.

What's wrong with the following sentence?

That conversation had a powerful affect on Gordon.

Affect is not the word you need; *effect* is correct. *Affect* as a noun means "emotion" or "mood"; *effect* as a noun means "an outcome or result." *Affect* as a verb means "to influence," whereas *effect* as a verb means "to cause to occur."

There are many such tricky pairs in English. Since a varied and properly used vocabulary will raise your score, you should work to sharpen your vocabulary.

If you have a spare hour, log on to **www.sparknotes.com/ultimatestyle** and check out our book *SparkNotes Ultimate Style* for a comprehensive list of commonly misused words.

Idioms and Prepositional Idioms

Idioms are inherited quirks of language that we absorb without question but which cause nonnative speakers endless trouble.

For example, here's an idiom we've all used:

It wasn't me.

Look at this grammatically. A pronoun that refers only to humans, *me*, is replacing a pronoun that refers only to inanimate objects, *it*. However, every native English-speaker knows what this phrase means, and has used it quite effectively.

These types of idioms are so dangerously close to clichés that you should avoid them at all costs.

However, the proper use of another type of idiom will definitely impress your readers. The particular meaning of certain words requires the use of a particular preposition:

Incorrect: Helga prefers poetry over novels.
Correct: Helga prefers poetry to novels.

Incorrect: Barack doesn't have a favorable opinion toward Freud's theories.

Correct: Barack doesn't have a favorable opinion of Freud's theories.

Sometimes, a word can be combined legitimately with more than one preposition, but the meaning will then shift. Knowing which preposition triggers which meaning is crucial to good usage.

My remark was meant **as** a joke.
You, my friend, are meant **for** greatness.

Meant as shows intent; *meant for* indicates a destination. A complete and relatively short list of such **prepositional idioms** can also be found in *SparkNotes Ultimate Style* (**www.sparknotes.com/ultimatestyle**).

Double Negatives
Finally, let's consider **double negatives**. When we want to negate something, we use *no* or *not:*

I allow **no** talking during a movie.
I do **not** allow talking during a movie.

For reasons of redundancy and idiomatic preference, we don't use both *no* and *not* in the same sentence:

I do **not** allow **no** talking during a movie.

Words other than *no* and *not* can indicate negation. Here's a list of those words with their positive counterparts (which are not necessarily their **antonyms**). Don't use a negative word with *not* or *no*.

Negative Word	Positive Counterpart	Examples
never	ever	**Incorrect:** I don't never eat meat. **Correct:** I never eat meat. **Correct:** I don't ever eat meat.
none	any	**Incorrect:** I don't want none. **Correct:** I want none. **Correct:** I don't want any.

neither	either	**Incorrect:** I don't want neither of those two puppies. **Correct:** I want neither of those two puppies. **Correct:** I don't want either of those two puppies.
nor	or	**Incorrect:** I don't want the puppy nor the kitten. **Correct:** I want neither the puppy nor the kitten. **Correct:** I don't want the puppy or the kitten.
nothing	anything	**Incorrect:** I don't want nothing from you. **Correct:** I want nothing from you. **Correct:** I don't want anything from you.
no one	anyone	**Incorrect:** I can't help no one. **Correct:** I can help no one. **Correct:** I can't help anyone.
nobody	anybody	**Incorrect:** I don't know nobody here. **Correct:** I know nobody here. **Correct:** I don't know anybody here.
nowhere	anywhere	**Incorrect:** I can't go nowhere with this cast on my leg. **Correct:** I can go nowhere with this cast on my leg. **Correct:** I can't go anywhere with this cast on my leg.

Three other words are often involved in double negatives: *hardly, scarcely,* and *barely.*

I can't hardly wait to graduate. (Two negatives—*can't* and *hardly*)

Believe it or not, this is not grammatically incorrect. But it has fallen into extreme idiomatic disfavor. Do not use these words in your essay! Instead, use:

I can hardly wait to graduate. (One negative—*hardly*)
I can't wait to graduate. (One negative—*can't*)

Now that you have all these concepts under your belt, it's time to learn the most effecient way to use your knowledge on the SAT essay.

ESSENTIAL STRATEGIES

The scoring rubric rewards essays that are:

- Well organized
- Well supported
- Well written

These goals are related but somewhat separable. Since you only have 25 minutes to achieve these three goals, it makes sense to split them up. That's where our step method comes in.

TACKLING THE ESSAY

Use this five-step method when tackling the essay:

Step 1: Read and interpret the prompt.

Step 2: Brainstorm.

Step 3: Outline.

Step 4: Write.

Step 5: Proof/Edit.

We're going to detail each step to show you how you can achieve a well-organized, well-supported, and well-written essay. But first, some suggestions for how to break up your 25 minutes among each step:

Step	Suggested Time (Minutes)
Read and interpret the prompt.	1
Brainstorm.	3–4
Outline.	2–3

Step	Suggested Time (Minutes)
Write.	around 15
Proof/Edit.	1–2

Note that these times aren't exact. A prompt that requires more brain-storming—say, on something you've never considered before—might need a minute more; a prompt for which you have almost too much to say might require an extra minute or so for the outline.

The more you practice this method, the quicker you'll get at each step and the more time you'll have for step 4, the writing. Notice, too, how this method separates the achievement of the three goals into separate tasks:

Goal	Step
Organization	Steps 1, 2, and 3
Support	
Writing	Steps 4 and 5

Let's look at each step in depth to see how each prevents typical errors and advances you toward your goals.

Tackling the Essay Step by Step

Step 1: Read and interpret the prompt (1 minute).

Prompts, as you now know, are written in purposely general terms. The SAT wants to make these prompts open to as many different types of answers as possible. To make sense of the prompt, you need to consider the terms being used. For example, if the prompt asks about "freedom of speech," you first have to determine what that term means to you. Is it the freedom to say whatever you want whenever you want, or is it the freedom to say whatever you want so long as it doesn't harm another person? Also, in defining the terms, you'll be working toward your **thesis statement**, which is a one-sentence explanation of your position or point of view.

Step 2: Brainstorm (3–4 minutes).

Brainstorming means using the space beneath the prompt to jot down a few ideas that come to mind. Depending on the prompt, you may know exactly which position you'd like to take.

In that case, start listing reasons and examples. However, you might not know which side of the argument you want to take. If you find yourself in this situation, use a T-chart to organize your brainstorming. Here's an example:

Pro	Con
reason	reason
example	example
reason	reason

And so on.

Brainstorming helps you decide what position to take and what ideas and examples will support it. You'll generate your thesis statement here, after you've chosen which side to take. These are important features of the scoring rubric.

You'll soon get a chance to use a T-chart in our slow-motion example.

Step 3: Outline (2–3 minutes).

The number one mistake you can make is not to take at least a couple of minutes to create an outline. Organization is one of the key criteria by which you'll be judged. The outline is where you select and arrange your supporting reasons and the examples that back them up.

Your outline does not have to be pretty. Your outline should match the final structure of your essay:

I. Intro
   A. Thesis statement
   B. Reasons for thesis statement
II. Reason 1
   A. Example/evidence in support
   B. Example/evidence in support
   C. Example/evidence in support
III. Reason 2
   A. Example/evidence in support
   B. Example/evidence in support
   C. Example/evidence in support
IV. Reason 3
   A. Example/evidence in support
   B. Example/evidence in support
   C. Example/evidence in support
V. Conclusion
   A. Restate—but don't repeat—thesis statement
   B. Expand thesis to larger point or relate to another area
      (optional)

Now, some very important points about the outline. Let's do it as a Q & A:

Q. Do I have to have a thesis statement?

A. Yes. That shows that you've taken a position, that you have a point of view, and that you're thinking about the prompt *critically*.

Q. Should I introduce all my reasons in my intro paragraph?

A. Yes. It builds out the paragraph, introduces what's to come (which lays out a "map" for the flow for your readers), and it can also flesh out your thesis statement.

Q. Do I have to have three reasons and three examples or pieces of evidence?

A. No. You can have two reasons, each of which has four examples. But you must have at least two reasons, and they must be well supported. You can also have only two pieces of evidence for each reason if you have three reasons, but avoid having more than three reasons, as you'll likely run out of time or insufficiently support one or more of the reasons.

Q. Do I have to have a conclusion?

A. Yes. Round out your structure by restating the thesis. Do *not* use the same words—remember, vocabulary variety is part of the scoring rubric.

Q. Is expanding my thesis to a larger point really optional?

A. Yes. If you're sure you've covered everything, you'll add this later, as you'll see below.

Step 4: Write (around 15 minutes).

OK, steps 1, 2, and 3 took care of creating the kind of support and organization you need to impress your readers. Time to turn to issues of writing. By this, we mean all the concepts we introduced in the Essential Concepts section. Your job is to make sure your language is as clear, varied, and forceful as possible.

Organization and support are taken care of; you don't need to worry about *what* you're going to write, but *how* you're going to write it. Concentrate on clarity, variation of sentence structure and vocabulary, and the transitions between sentences and paragraphs.

We'll practice this together in a moment.

Step 5: Proof/Edit (1–2 minutes).

Don't blow off this step unless you're *really* pressed for time. Catching and fixing writing errors and adding new thoughts that might come up will raise your score. You won't necessarily come up with new thoughts to change your essay, but leave a minute or so just in case.

If you've covered everything, and you feel you have a decent way to expand your thesis or relate it to another area, go ahead. But this is optional. We'll show you an example of a legitimate expansion shortly.

Tackling the Essay in Slow Motion

You're now ready to work through an entire SAT essay experience.

This will *not* be timed; we're working on method now, not speed. If this takes you up to about an hour, as opposed to exactly 25 minutes, that's fine. In order to demonstrate the step method in action, we'll do this essay in slow motion, making all thought processes explicit.

We want your practice to be as realistic as possible. So before you start this exercise, do the following:

- **Prepare essay sheets.** Get two sheets of college-ruled 8 1/2"-by-11" paper. That's about the size of your actual Student Response Sheet.

Count off about 50 lines and give yourself left and right margins of about a half inch each. That's about the size you'll be given. We'll refer to these sheets of paper as *essay sheets* throughout the exercise.

- **Give yourself some planning space.** In addition to the 50 lines above, give yourself about two-thirds of a separate sheet of paper to plan your essay. We'll refer to this sheet of paper as the *planning space* throughout the exercise.
- **Use the two-column method.** We suggest that you separate your planning space into two columns. Use the left column for steps 1 and 2, defining terms and brainstorming. Use the right for step 3, outlining. You're much less likely to run out of space for your outline that way.

We'll let you do the steps on your own. After you've completed each step, we'll show you our version for comparison.

When you're all set, start with step 1 below.

Step 1: Read and interpret the prompt.

On the following page is that prompt from the beginning of the book. Read it carefully.

Essay Prompt:

Think carefully about the issue presented in the quotations and the assignment below.

1. *Technological progress, while often beneficial, has nevertheless outpaced human social and ethical development. We lack the wisdom to manage these increasingly dangerous tools.*
> —Adapted from Hugh B. Riis, *"Techno-hazard"*

2. *The past four centuries have seen the greatest improvement of the human condition in history. Technological progress, while not without its pitfalls, holds out the possibility of achieving a healthier and more humane society in which people lead richer and longer lives than were ever thought possible.*
> —Editorial, *"Technology: The Way Forward"*

Assignment: Is technology dangerous, or does it provide a way to solve our problems? Plan and write an essay in which you develop your position on this issue. Support your point of view with reasoning and examples taken from your reading, studies, experience, or observations.

In the left column of your planning space, jot down how you interpret or define *technology* and *progress.*

Also, are you sure you know what *ethical development* and *human social development* mean? How about the *human condition*? Define them if they seem too broad.

Don't try to be "deep"; just think a little and start refining these terms if they're not clear.

Don't worry about taking a few minutes to work this out. The skill of interpreting the prompt is critical to all the rest of the steps in this method. You'll get faster as you practice.

Our Version

Notice that each quote is balanced. Quote 1, which is mostly against technological progress, admits that it's *often beneficial.* Quote 2, which is mostly for technological progress, notes that it's *not without its pitfalls.*

This kind of measured terminology is not uncommon and shouldn't throw you. The SAT is just trying to make the prompt as answerable in as wide a range of ways as possible, without prejudicing any test-taker one way or the other (pro or con).

Here's how we interpreted the quotes:

- Quote 1 maintains that we humans haven't caught up morally to our technological power (*technological progress . . . has outpaced human social and ethical development . . .*). Therefore, we're not wise enough to manage these tools.
- Quote 2 says that even though technology has its dangers, it's still the best hope for improving human life.

Here's how we defined our terms:

- We defined *technology* as "modern machinery or technical processes, like nuclear energy, cars, the Internet, genetic engineering, or medicine."
- We defined *progress* as "when more and more people's lives are made better and better."

You may have defined these terms differently—no big deal. But these are examples of what you have to do to make the prompt "answerable" and to display your ability to think critically.

Remember, there's no right or wrong answer here. Unlike a history or literature essay test, you don't have to provide any absorbed facts. The SAT essay is the ultimate open-book test: you can literally "make up" your answer!

Finally, don't worry about handwriting in the planning space—that's all for you. You're graded only on the essay itself.

Step 2: Brainstorm.

Make a T-chart like the below in the left column of your planning space to generate ideas and examples (i.e., evidence) you can use for either side to see which one you'd like to do:

Pro	Con

When you're done, generate a thesis statement. This doesn't have to be beautifully written; you'll have time for that in step 4: writing.

Feel free to take a few minutes or more to brainstorm. We want you to internalize this method; there'll be plenty of time to get faster once you know how to do it.

Read on when you're ready.

Our Version

We didn't feel we had a clear opinion one way or the other; we saw both sides of the issue. So we made a T-chart and started scribbling down reasons and examples:

Pro Tech	Con Tech
longer life spans	more people—can't support them all; ecological stress; fewer resources; more wars
medicines, better health care, public health	weapons of mass destruction
more art/entertainment: TV, Internet, video games, electric instruments, travel	accidents from WMDs or from nuclear power
more wealth—computers and business, more jobs	global warming; environmental destruction; new diseases traveling around the world
more time to do more things as travel and computers get cheaper	threat of altering ourselves genetically
	loss of privacy—surveillance technology
	less quiet time—more stress

Looks like we've got more material on the "con" side, so we'll go with that. Go with the side that has the most material. You're judged on how well you support your argument, not what side you take.

Here's our quick-and-dirty thesis statement:

Technology, while not totally negative, causes more problems than it solves, and should therefore be controlled.

Not pretty, but it describes a position/point of view.

Step 3: Outline.

Use the right side of your planning space to jot down your outline.

You need to decide which of your brainstorming points are reasons, which are examples you can use as evidence, and which order to put them in.

Take the time you need to get the hang of creating an outline. Outlining is where a lot of the hardest writing work is done.

Use the model outline reproduced below for reference:

I. Intro
   A. Thesis statement
   B. Reasons for thesis statement
II. Reason 1
   A. Example/evidence in support
   B. Example/evidence in support
   C. Example/evidence in support
III. Reason 2
   A. Example/evidence in support
   B. Example/evidence in support
   C. Example/evidence in support
IV. Reason 3
   A. Example/evidence in support
   B. Example/evidence in support
   C. Example/evidence in support
V. Conclusion
   A. Restate—but don't repeat—thesis statement
   B. Expand thesis to larger point or relate to another area
      (optional)

Read our version when you're done.

Our Version

Pay attention to both sides of your brainstorming chart when creating an outline, as sometimes a positive statement can help you form an argument against it. For example, one of our reasons will be that longer life spans, due to better medical technology, are causing a population explosion.

Here's our thesis statement:

Technology, while not totally negative, causes more problems than it solves, and should therefore be controlled.

And here's our outline:

I. Intro
   A. Thesis statement
   B. Reasons for thesis statement
II. Medical advances cause population explosion
   A. More people mean fewer resources; more wars: oil wars in middle east
   B. More people mean more travel (made easier by tech) and spread of disease
   C. Coming genetic alteration of humanity; eugenics becoming possible
III. Ecological stress
   A. Fewer resources as population grows—oil
   B. Global warming as more people burn fossil fuels
   C. Environmental destruction killing species
IV. Imminent dangers
   A. WMDs—technology spreading; terrorism; accident
   B. New diseases from rise in population and travel: HIV, Ebola
   C. Loss of privacy as terrorism rises; end of democracy?
V. Conclusion
   A. Restate—but don't repeat—thesis statement
   B. Expand thesis to larger point or relate to another area (optional)—end of democracy?

Note a few things about our outline:

- We thought of more evidence as we made the outline. That's to be expected and is a good thing! Furthermore, we didn't use everything from our brainstorm. You don't have to shove it all in. As you make decisions on structure, via the outlining process, you'll discard some ideas and include new ones.
- We only filled in the middle paragraphs with actual reasons and their supporting evidence. Why? To save time—we already know that the first paragraph will contain a thesis statement and introduction, and that the last paragraph will restate the thesis statement and maybe expand it a bit.
- We put one idea—*end of democracy*—in two places. You don't have to make *every* decision up front in the outline. We may use this idea in either of two places, or we may chuck it. We'll find out as we write.

- We wrote this out more completely than you would. Your outline probably looked more notelike than ours. That's fine. Only *you* need to understand it.

Step 4: Write.

Use your essay sheet to write your essay. Refer to your outline: follow that structure and don't make any changes to the structure in the middle of your writing. You've thought through your structure: trust that structure. Now concentrate on using the clearest, most correct, and most varied language you can to express your ideas.

You don't have to limit yourself to around 15 minutes for now—there'll be plenty of opportunity for that. But don't go on forever! Develop your outline into a reasonable first draft and stop.

After you're done, read on to check out our version.

Our Version

We haven't proofed or edited yet, so we'll discuss this essay in detail later. For now, just read what we've written and compare it to your own essay.

Remember, *what* you (or we) wrote about doesn't matter at all. *How* we structured and supported the argument and how well we used language are all that matters.

While modern technology has given humanity many benefits, it has caused more problems than it has solved. In the last century, amazing advances in medicine and public health have extended the average human life span. However, the resulting population explosion has had all kinds of problems. Furthermore, these problems have led to new dangers with which we may not be able to cope, and which might lead to the end of our way of life.

Medical technologies, such as antibiotics and anasthesia, and better public health standards have extended life. While that might seem like a good thing, the world's population is out of control. All of these people are competing for the same resources, which is leading to increased conflict. For example, two wars have already been fought in the middle east at least in part over oil. Wars over resources will only increase as population rises. Furthermore, the increasing population is driving deeper into uninhabited areas, encountering new diseases, like HIV and Ebola. As international travel becomes more widespread, these diseases break out and cause new epidemics against which medicine is sometimes powerless. Finally, cutting-edge genetic technologies seem to be as dangerous as they are beneficial.

In fact, it's not true that an increasing number of people are competing for the same resources. The amount of some resources is actually shrinking. Again, oil is a good example. At some point soon, we will run out of this fuel which supports our entire economy. Similarly, the world's forests are being cut down at an alarming rate. As more fuel is burned, global warming is actually changing the Earth's climate. Finally, as population rises and uses up resources, environmental destruction is killing off large number of species.

If all this weren't bad enough, some dangers facing our world stem directly from technology. First, weapons of mass destruction are spreading to other countries, and possibly even to terrorists. Second, these terrorists already use some of our other technologies, such as the Internet and airplanes, against us. As we work to battle the spread of terrorism, we are using sophisticated surveillance technologies. Will the use of these technologies lead to the end of our free way of life? Or will terrorists use other technologies, such as weapons of mass destruction, to cause us even greater harm?

It seems that technology creates new problems as it solves old ones. Perhaps humankind should consider pausing for a moment and thinking about whether we've matured to the point where we can handle the technologies we've created.

Step 5: Proof/Edit.

Go ahead and look over your essay now. Keep your eye out for the following:

- Language errors you can quickly, easily, and legibly fix.
- Any opportunity to clarify or add to your argument, if it can be done quickly and legibly.
- Any opportunity to remove confusion or incoherence in your essay, if it can be done quickly and legibly.

The key here is to polish, not reconstruct. Don't make things worse—especially by making your essay less readable—but if you see something you can fix or improve quickly, clearly, and easily, go for it.

Even though we're in "slow-motion" mode now, only take a couple of minutes for this step. We'll show you some examples of improvements to our essay on the next page.

Read on when you're ready.

Our Version

We're going to make a few changes using ~~strikethroughs~~ for deletions and **bold** for additions. We'll number each change (also in **bold)** and discuss them below the essay, along with some general points we'd like to highlight.

While modern technology has given humanity many benefits, it has caused more problems than it has solved. In the last century, amazing advances in medicine and public health have extended the average human life span. However, the resulting population explosion has had all kinds of problems. Furthermore, these **[1]** ~~problems~~ **consequences** have led to new dangers with which we may not be able to cope, and which might lead to the end of our way of life.

Medical technologies, such as antibiotics and anasthesia, and better public health standards have extended life. While these might seem like a good thing, the world's population is out of control. All of these people are competing for the same resources, which is leading to increased conflict. For example, two wars have already been fought in the **[2]** ~~middle east~~ Middle East at least in part over oil. Wars over resources will only increase as population rises. Furthermore, the **[3]** ~~increasing~~ population is ~~driving deeper~~ **spreading** into uninhabited areas, encountering new diseases, like HIV and Ebola. As international travel becomes more widespread, these diseases **[4]** ~~break out and~~ cause new epidemics against which medicine is sometimes powerless. Finally, cutting-edge genetic technologies seem to be as dangerous as they are beneficial.

In fact, it's not true that an increasing number of people are competing for the same resources. The amount of some resources is actually shrinking. Again, oil is a good example. At some point soon, we will run out of this fuel **[5]** ~~which~~ **that** supports our entire economy.

Similarly, the world's forests are being cut down at an alarming rate. As **[6] we burn** more fuel ~~is burned~~, global warming is actually changing the Earth's climate. Finally, as population rises and uses up resources, environmental destruction is killing off large number of species.

If all this weren't bad enough, some dangers facing our world stem directly from technology. First, weapons of mass destruction are spreading to other countries, and possibly even to terrorists. Second, these terrorists already use **[7]** ~~some of our~~ other technologies, such as the Internet and airplanes, against us. As we work to battle the spread of terrorism, we are using sophisticated surveilance technologies. Will the use of these technologies lead to the end of our free way of life? Or will terrorists use other technologies, such as weapons of mass destruction, to cause us even greater harm?

It seems that technology creates new problems **[8] even** as it solves old ones. Perhaps humankind should consider pausing for a moment **[9] to consider** ~~and thinking about~~ whether **we have the maturity** ~~we've matured~~ to ~~the point where we can~~ handle **these** ~~the~~ technologies ~~we've created~~.

---

[1] : Notice that we repeated *problems*. We changed one to a synonym, *consequences,* increasing vocabulary variety.

[2] : *Middle East* is a proper noun. It should be capitalized.

[3]: First, we noticed that we used the word *increasing* (or some form of it) a lot. So we cut it here since it's clear that the population we're talking about is *rising,* as the previous sentence states. Second, the phrase *driving deeper* seemed awkward when we read it. Anything awkward interrupts the flow of your writing, which is a big no-no. So, we substituted a simpler construction: in this case, a well-chosen and clear verb.

[4] : Cutting is easier and quicker to do than adding, Since being redundant obscures meaning and being concise is very important, don't hesitate to scribble out needless words. *Break out and* wasn't necessary.

[5] : *That* is usually better than *which.* We noticed that we use a lot of *which* clauses in this essay, and why use a *which* when you don't really need one? Variation also played a role in this decision.

[6] : We changed a passive construction to an active one. That improves the flow and coherence and makes the essay more concise—all in one fell swoop.

[7] : Made that cut for the same reason as **[4]**. Trim what fat you can, as time permits.

[8] : The inclusion of this word focused the flow a bit more, giving a picture of well-meant technologies giving rise to new problems as they solve old ones.

[9] : The last sentence needed work. We're assuming we had the time to do this—as well as all of these corrections. We substituted a forceful infinitive (*to consider*) for a weak gerund (*and thinking about*— watch out for that weak *and*; it can show up like this, too!). We then cut a slew of words in the *maturity* phrase to make the point more concisely and forcefully. Finally, it's understood that *we* are human beings, and *we* human beings created this technology. No need for those last two words.

Reviewing the Slow-Motion Essay Experience

The Small Stuff

Note that we didn't catch every single error.

- We misspelled *surveillance* as *surveilance* and *anesthesia* as *anasthesia* in the original and in our final version. So what? Readers will forgive a couple of misspelled words, especially if they're toughies.
- We used *finally* at the end of two paragraphs. That's not great.
- The phrase *if all this weren't bad enough* is a little clunky. It could've been done better.

Don't worry about catching everything: you're writing a **first draft**! (Have we mentioned this before?) Our essay, by the way, would probably be considered a "high" 6. You'll see a variety of essays at different score levels in the practice section.

Tone

Note how we took a stand, but we did so with a respectful tone, pointing out the ironic, unintended consequences of well-meant technologies. We didn't present a conspiracy theory. The SAT likes balance because it tests *critical thinking.* And these prompts can be answered by reasonable people in any number of ways, pro or con. So note the world of difference between (1) having a position with a point of view and (2) simply writing dogmatically and unthinkingly. Dogma is very hard to support, anyway, especially in 25 minutes.

Position

Trust that the readers won't care what you write about, contentwise. Our sentence, *For example, two wars have already been fought in the Middle East at least in part over oil* is pretty controversial. We put it in on purpose. Your readers are trained to ignore what you say; all they care about is *how* you say it. As written, this sentence is both evenhanded (*at least in part . . .*) and offers a reasonable piece of evidence for the argument, regardless of what anyone thinks about it.

This is a key point: don't try to "psych out" the readers. You know what they're looking for, who they are, how they're trained. Don't try to outsmart them: you can't, and you don't have to.

The Big Stuff

Here are some positive aspects of this essay that you should strive to emulate:

- Signpost words are used throughout to lead the reader from one sentence (which is really "one idea") to the next. The first paragraph is a good example of the proper use of signpost words and words that act as signposts (*however, furthermore*).
- Reasons support the thesis statement, whether you (or the readers) agree with the thesis or not.
- There are ample and appropriate examples to support each reason.
- There is a lot of variety in sentence structure and vocabulary. Look at each sentence in isolation to see how they vary in structure.
- Note how the outline determined the flow of the argument.
- Note how language enhances the flow in our outline structure. First, oil is *purposely* repeated as an example in two different paragraphs but is used differently and appropriately in each paragraph. Second, expanding population is shown to have several related consequences. Finally, after detailing eventual and potential threats posed by technology, the conclusion returns to the transition sentence in the first paragraph: *Furthermore, these consequences*

have led to new dangers with which we may not be able to cope, and which might lead to the end of our way of life.

Finally, keep in mind that our essay is a "high" 6. You can write a shorter, less sophisticated essay and still earn a 6 for your work, as you'll see in the practice sets.

THE 15 MOST COMMON MISTAKES

1. Diving right into writing without first *thinking* or *planning*. This is definitely *the* most common mistake.
2. Thinking that the longer your essay is, the higher your score will be, regardless of organization or use of language.
3. Not thoroughly understanding the scoring rubric and how readers will use it to score your essay. It all starts with the scoring rubric. The rubric determined the Essential Concepts we presented to you and formed the Essential Strategies and step method you've just learned.
4. Not *practicing* the step method—*reading* this book is not enough!
5. Not mastering the essential concepts, both of building a strong argument and of language.
6. Worrying about constructing the perfect argument expressed in perfect language. You're writing a first draft!
7. Not taking a particular position on the issue.
8. Not thoroughly supporting your position with an argument made up of well-chosen reasons and examples.
9. Not varying your sentence structure accurately and appropriately.
10. Using fancy-schmancy words inappropriately without knowing their precise meaning.
11. Deviating from your outline in the middle of writing your essay. Take the time to get your thoughts straight before writing.
12. "Overwriting"—using highfalutin sentences incorrectly. You won't impress anyone. Vary your sentences, but vary them appropriately and correctly.

13. Being "cute." Don't aim to be boring, but don't take any chances with structure or language on the essay. *Structured* does not equal *boring.*

14. Writing on another topic. That will get you a score of zero.

15. Writing illegibly. That will also get you a score of zero.

CONCLUSION

You've learned quite a bit in reading this book. You now know:

- The structure and purpose of the SAT essay.
- How essay-readers are selected and trained.
- The scoring rubric, and how to use it to your advantage.
- How to construct a well-supported argument.
- Which language errors to avoid.
- Which features of language essay-readers will reward.
- A step method that provides a way to break up the writing process efficiently.

It's now time to apply what you've learned to some sample essays. To that end, we provide you with some practice in the next section. First, you'll be shown a sample essay prompt and six responses. *You* will score each response, according to your new knowledge of the scoring rubric and holistic scoring. Then, we'll tell you the scores of each essay and explain how they were scored.

We'll then provide you with several prompts you can use for practice. Since you're now quite familiar with the scoring rubric and what is expected of you, you can score your own essays.

Scoring essays is a great way to practice. By effectively using the scoring rubric to grade your own writing, you'll begin to think like an essay-reader. And the more you think like an essay-reader, the more likely you'll produce a 6 essay.

AND FINALLY . . .

We've attempted to make this book as useful as possible for helping you prepare for the SAT essay. The writing you've learned may be a bit formulaic, but it's the basis of more creative, more rewarding writing experiences. The ability to write well is a rare and marketable skill—and a great pleasure.

We wish you the best of luck!

THE PRACTICE
SETS

TURNING THE TABLES

PLAY SAT ESSAY-READER

We've said this before, but it's worth repeating: by learning how to grade SAT essays, you will train yourself to write an essay that matches the essay-readers' expectations.

Read the following essay prompt:

Think carefully about the following incomplete statement. Then read the assignment below it and plan and write your essay as directed.

"I have learned many things from many experiences, but I have never learned as much as when I ___."

Assignment: Plan and write an essay in which you complete the statement above by selecting an event or experience from your life.

We will provide you with six responses to this prompt.

We will provide both the "distilled" and complete scoring rubrics below. Use these to score each response *holistically*. If you like, you may reread the sections How Is the Essay Scored and How Essay-Readers Apply the Scoring Rubric (pp. 20–28). When you're ready to score, skip to page 88 for the responses.

After you've scored the responses, you'll get a chance to compare your scores with ours and to read our scoring rationales.

First, here's the "distilled" version of the scoring rubric:

Score	6	5	4
Features	General overall impression		
	Point of view; critical thinking; examples, reasons, and evidence		
	Organization, focus, coherence, and flow		
	Vocabulary and use of language		
	Sentence structure		
	Errors in grammar and usage		

Score	3	2	1
Features	General overall impression		
	Point of view; critical thinking; examples, reasons, and evidence		
	Organization, focus, coherence, and flow		
	Vocabulary and use of language		
	Sentence structure		
	Errors in grammar and usage		

Remember, first the essay-readers focus on holistic grading—their overall impression—and decide if an essay is in the top (4, 5, 6) or bottom (1, 2, 3) of the rubric. Then they decide what the score is within each half. Here is the complete scoring rubric to guide your decision:

General Overall Impression	
Score Level	**Defining Characteristics**
6	An exceptional essay that shows sustained expertise, but which contains a few minor errors
5	A successful essay that shows mostly sustained expertise, even though it contains occasional mistakes or slips in quality
4	An adequate essay that shows competence, but which contains more than occasional mistakes or slips in quality
3	An insufficient essay that shows signs of evolving competence and features one or more specific flaws

General Overall Impression	
Score Level	**Defining Characteristics**
2	A weak essay that shows serious limitations, insufficient facility, and which features one or more specific flaws
1	An essentially deficient essay that displays fundamental inability and features severe manifestations of one or more specific flaws
0	No essay written Essay that doesn't respond to the assignment An illegible essay

Point of View; Critical Thinking; Examples, Reasons, and Evidence	
Score Level	**Defining Characteristics**
6	Impressively insightful point of view Outstanding critical thinking Completely appropriate reasons, examples, and evidence to support point of view
5	Well-developed point of view Strong critical thinking Generally appropriate reasons, examples, and evidence to support point of view
4	Fairly well developed point of view Adequate critical thinking Mostly appropriate reasons, examples, and evidence to support point of view
3	Develops a point of view Some evidence of critical thinking, but inconsistently apparent Sometimes inappropriate reasons, examples, and evidence to support point of view
2	Develops a vague point of view Little evidence of critical thinking Insufficient or inappropriate reasons, examples, and evidence to support point of view

Point of View; Critical Thinking; Examples, Reasons, and Evidence	
Score Level	**Defining Characteristics**
1	Does not develop a point of view No evidence of critical thinking Little or no evidence to support point of view

Organization, Focus, Coherence, and Flow	
Score Level	**Defining Characteristics**
6	Well organized Tightly focused Tight coherence Smooth flow of ideas
5	Well organized Focused Coheres reasonably well Mostly smooth flow of ideas
4	Generally organized Generally focused Shows some coherence Discernable but not particularly smooth flow of ideas
3	Partially organized Partially unfocused Some incoherent portions Interrupted or disrupted flow of ideas
2	Poorly organized Mostly unfocused Systemic problems with incoherence Flow of ideas difficult to discern
1	Disorganized Unfocused Incoherent Flow of ideas impossible to discern or entirely absent

Vocabulary and Use of Language	
Score Level	Defining Characteristics
6	Skilled use of language Varied, accurate, and appropriate vocabulary
5	Capable use of language Appropriate vocabulary
4	Satisfactory but inconsistent use of language Generally appropriate vocabulary
3	Inconsistent use of language that shows signs of evolving competence Some inappropriate word choice; weak vocabulary
2	Insufficient use of language Very limited vocabulary or incorrect word choice
1	Basic vocabulary errors

Sentence Structure	
Score Level	Defining Characteristics
6	Displays meaningful variety
5	Displays variety
4	Displays some variety
3	Does not display variety Displays problems
2	Displays frequent problems
1	Displays serious and widespread problems

Errors in Grammar and Usage	
Score Level	Defining Characteristics
6	Free of most errors
5	On the whole, free of most errors
4	Has some errors
3	Has a lot of errors
2	Has so many errors that meaning is partially hidden
1	Persistent and widespread errors that obscure meaning

Finally, the responses, in no particular score order.

Essay A

I learned a lot about life during my summer as a camp counselor. I had been going to the camp as a camper since I was eight, but this time I was going to be a counselor. I had to lead activities and make sure the campers took care of themselves in the morning and at night. I also had to make sure they behaved themselves in the dinner hall.

One time a lot of the campers were misbahaving and not doing they're morning chores. The head counselor came in and discovered the chaos in the cabin. He singled out one camper who had done everything he should of and told the other campers that they should be more like Michael. When the head counselor left, all the other campers started making fun of Michael and called him a teacher's pet. Michael got very upset and told me he wanted to leave camp and go back home. I learned that being singled out sometimes makes you feel bad even if it is for something good. I told Michael that he should ignore what the other kids saying and stay at camp because things would get better. And they did!

That summer I learned that singling someone out for something good can make them unpopular. I also learned that situations can improve if you just stick with it.

Your Score:

Essay B

The question of what is the experience you have learned the most from seems like an important question to me. After all, learning is very important and is the reason I am here right now. What is college about if not to learn. In order to get a job you first have to learn about the world and aquire knowledge so thats why you have to go to school for four years first. Of course, you can learn in other places as well. In fact almost anything could be considered a learning experience if you aproach it in the right way.

Your Score:

Essay C

I have never learned as much as when I try something new for the first time. When you do something you already know how to do, you are really just repeating the knowledge you already have. It is only when you do something you have never done before that you actually learn. The first day of school, the first day of a job, your first time going rock-climbing—these are all learning experiences. You learn new skills, discover more about yourself, meet new people etc. Usually you aren't very good the first you try something but practice makes perfect as they say. I always try to do something new when I have the chance. Learning new things helps you develop as a person, and always gives you a sense of fulfilment. Usually it is hard to do something new and you can easily become discouraged. What you have to think about is that next time everything will be easier. Learning is what life is really all about. At the end, you can judge how well you lived by how much you learned. If you have learned alot that means you have had a successful life and should be satisfied with what you have done.

Your Score:

Essay D

You wouldn't think you could learn much from a karate class apart from how to defend yourself, but I certainly did. Karate gave me so much respect for myself. I truly believe I would have turned out a very different person if I had not started taking karate lessons at the age of twelve.

From the very first class, my teacher taught me the importance of wearing a clean, properly arranged uniform. I had to learn how to tie my belt in the traditional way and also how to keep it in place while doing all the exercises. If the belt comes undone, you are supposed to turn around to face the back of the class while you retie it. If you look presentable, other people will respect you, but in order to look presentable you first have to respect yourself.

If you do poorly in an exercise, you can't just feel sorry for yourself or cry like a baby. You have to put on a bold face and concentrate on doing well the next time. Nobody is going to help you if you don't help yourself, so it is very important to do your best all the time. One time the kid next to me got punched in the nose. Screaming in pain, with blood running down his chin, I couldn't believe how much pain he was in just because he didn't pay attention when he should of. This taught me how important it is to concentrate and not let yourself get distracted.

All in all, taking karate lessons taught me about alot more than just how to defend myself. It taught me how to take care of my uniform and make myself presentable. It taught me that not paying attention can get you into much worse trouble than just being told off by the teacher. I learned so much in karate that I'm glad me parents signed me up for it, even though I wasn't crazy about getting started at the time.

Your Score:

Essay E

The most meaningful learning experience of my life occurred when I helped my friend Keiko draft her first essay in English. I expected to learn a lot about Japanese culture while helping Keiko write about moving from Japan to America. What I did not expect, however, was how much I would learn about my own culture. Additionally, I was surprised by what I learned about being teacher and the experience of working in unfamiliar surroundings.

Keiko grew up in Tokyo, a city I had always assumed was similar to New York, my hometown and Keiko's home for three months. Keiko wrote about how, in Tokyo, even though it is considered a faux pas if you bump into another person on the street, people don't mind being jostled on the crowded subway system. I realized that New Yorkers tend to follow the same behavior and expect the same sort of response from others in similar situations. What makes New York special is the attitude people display and expect others to display whatever the situation. Whether you are walking through a quiet part of Central Park or struggling through a crowd on Wall Street, people think nothing of it if you bump into them, provided that you say "Excuse Me."

Teaching Keiko how to write in English showed me how much one can lean about a subject just through the act of teaching. Helping Keiko understand the principles of English forced me to examine many grammatical rules I had never really understood before. For example, I never fully understood how to use a semicolon before researching the subject with Keiko. I truly believe that I learned as much about English as Keiko did from our lessons.

I also learned that, in the process of completing the assignment, Keiko faced challenges beyond those posed by learning the rules of English. If Keiko wanted to listen to the radio, she couldn't tune in to her favorite Tokyo music station. If she got hungry, she couldn't ask her mother to make her favorite Japanese snack. Even doing research for her essay was a challenge—Japanese libraries are set up differently from American ones, and Keiko had to familiarize herself with a new system before she could find what she needed.

All things considered, becoming a teacher to a friend in need was the most educational experience of my life. Having faced some of the challenges they confront everyday, I have a newfound respect for teachers and I hope to continue teaching throughout my life.

Your Score:

Essay F

I have learned form many experiences, but never as much as when I read *Moby-Dick*. In this story, Captain Ahab learns that you can't take revenge on an animal. Captain Ahab wants to take revenge on Moby Dick for biting off his leg, but even if he kills Moby Dick he wont have revenge. Moby Dick doesn't know who Captain Ahab is so he wont know he is getting revenge if he kills him. Lots of the other characters in the book are interesting. Captain Ahabs crew is made up of lots of different types of people, and them getting to know each other is something that makes the book interesting. All things considered, I have never learnt as much as I did when I read *Moby-Dick*. English class is worthwhile when you get to read such interesting stuff. Not everything is interesting, but *Moby-Dick* certainly was.

Your Score:

OUR SCORES AND SCORING RATIONALE

Please note: for the purposes of this exercise, we gave scores from 1–6, rather than the 2–12 which combines the scores of two readers on the actual SAT.

Essay A

- **Your Score** _____
- **Our Score** 4

This student addresses the writing task with a mostly appropriate and fairly comprehensible response. This essay shows some organization but little in the way of advance planning. The first paragraph introduces the scene of the learning experience but does not prepare the reader for any of the lessons it produced. The middle of the essay recounts just one moment, though the writer draws two lessons from it. Because the focus is on the experience itself, however, the reader has to wait until the conclusion to understand the second lesson. The thesis statement is not easy to identify.

The writer shows an adequate understanding of the conventions of written English but makes several errors. In the first sentence of the second paragraph, the word *misbehaving* is misspelled, and the contraction *they're* is written for the possessive pronoun *their*. In the seventh sentence of this paragraph, a word is omitted. While these kinds of mistakes make the comprehension more difficult for the reader, they do not obscure the writer's meaning. Although sentences are generally short and simple, the writer shows the ability to use the comma correctly.

Essay B

- **Your Score** _____
- **Our Score** 1

This student addresses the writing task in only the most cursory and glancing manner. The response is disorganized, with sentences following each other in a way that suggests no sense of direction. There are no specific or detailed examples and therefore there is no meaningful development.

Sentences are poorly constructed, with no sense of advance planning, making the response difficult to understand. Words are included or repeated for no apparent reason, which adds to the reader's confusion.

Simple words are misspelled, and apostrophes and other punctuation points are omitted, suggesting that the student is not familiar with the conventions of written English.

Essay C

- **Your Score** _____
- **Our Score** 3

This student addresses the prompt with a haphazard and confused response. This essay shows no evidence of purposeful organization. The response is clumped together into one paragraph, even though many of the sentences do not follow logically from the ones that precede them. The writer never gives a specific example of a learning experience, instead simply citing situations that could lead to the acquisition of new knowledge, skills, or acquaintances. The idea that the writer is trying to convey is clear, but there is no real development of this idea beyond the form it takes at its introduction

The writer shows familiarity with some of the conventions of written English but makes frequent errors. Commas are omitted or misplaced, and words are misspelled and sometimes omitted. These errors, together with the lack of organization, make the response difficult to follow. Sentences all have the same length and structure, and word choice is predictable.

Essay D

- **Your Score** _____
- **Our Score** 5

This student addresses the writing task with a clear and relevant response. The essay is organized into paragraphs but does not show as much careful planning as an essay that would receive the top score. The introduction raises the topic of self-respect but does not mention any of the other lessons set forth later in the essay. The central two paragraphs contain useful information, but there are not as many examples as you would find in a top essay. The examples in this essay are not as well developed as they could be. The conclusion recaps the points made in the body of the essay, but does not develop the thesis beyond the form it took in the introduction.

Sentences vary in length and structure but occasionally stray from the standards of written English. There is some variety of vocabulary, but also some mistakes in this area. The fifth sentence of the third paragraph begins with a dangling modifier ("Screaming in pain, with blood running down **his** chin, I . . ."), and ends with incorrect word usage (*"should of"* instead of *"should have"*). Also, in the first sentence of the fourth paragraph, the student writes *"alot"* instead of *"a lot."* These mistakes are noticeable but do not significantly interfere with the reader's understanding of the ideas contained in the essay.

Essay E

- **Your Score** _____
- **Our Score** 6

This student addresses the writing task with an interesting and persuasive response. The essay is well organized and thoughtfully developed with several pieces of evidence. The introduction specifies that the writer learned about Japanese and American culture, the experience of teaching, and the challenge of working in an unfamiliar environment. These three lessons provide the subject matter for the essay's three central paragraphs. In each paragraph, detailed evidence is given to support the writer's thesis that this experience was very educational. In the conclusion, the writer restates the thesis but also develops it with the idea that the experience has made teaching a lifelong pursuit for him or her.

Sentences vary in length and structure, which makes the essay easy to follow. The writer makes no significant errors in grammar or spelling and generally seems at ease with standard written English. Vocabulary is varied and words are well chosen for their purposes in conveying the writer's ideas.

Essay F

- **Your Score** _____
- **Our Score** 2

This student attempts to address the writing task but has trouble following the assignment. This response shows no attempt at organization. There is only one paragraph, and the conclusion comes in the seventh sentence; the last two sentences seem like afterthoughts added to engthen an insufficiently detailed response. The evidence is not entirely appropriate, since it details a fictional character's learning experience rather than one of the writer's own, and the writer strays completely off-topic in the fifth, sixth, eighth, and ninth sentences.

Although some sentences are constructed properly, others, such as the fourth sentence, are so poorly structured and punctuated that the writer's meaning is almost totally obscured. Otherwise, the writer seems familiar with the conventions of written English, although there are a few apostrophes omitted here and there. Word choice is sometimes imprecise and contributes to the difficulties with comprehension encountered by the reader.

PRACTICE ESSAY PROMPTS

Plan, write, and score your responses to these essays.

You may not want to give yourself a time limit on the first of the following essays you attempt. But note how long each step takes you. B the second or third practice essay, you should keep yourself to the following time limits:

Step	Suggested Time (Minutes)
Read and interpret the prompt.	1
Brainstorm.	3–4
Outline.	2–3
Write.	around 15
Proof/Edit.	1–2

Remember to construct your own Student Response Sheets. Get a normal-size pa of college-ruled 8 1/2"-by-11" paper. That's about the size of your actua Student Response Sheet. Count off about 50 lines and give yourself le and right margins of about a half inch each. That's about the size you' be given. You can use both sides of one sheet of paper, if you like, to be a realistic as possible.

Give yourself a reasonable amount of planning space. In addition to the 5 lines above, give yourself about two-thirds of a separate sheet of paper t plan your essay.

Don't forget the two-column method. We suggest that you separate you planning space into two columns. Use the left column for steps 1 and 2 lefining terms and brainstorming. Use the right for step 3, outlining. You're much less likely to run out of space for your outline that way.

1. <u>Essay Prompt</u>:

Think carefully about the following statement. Then read the assignment below it and plan and write your essay as directed.

"The more things change, the more they stay the same."

Assignment: Do you agree with this statement? Plan and write an essay in which you develop your position on this issue. Support your point of view with reasoning and examples taken from your reading, studies, experience, or observations.

2. <u>Essay Prompt</u>:

Consider carefully the following statement. Then read the assignment below it and plan and write your essay as directed.

"It is as difficult to start things as it is to finish things."

Assignment: Do you agree with this statement? Plan and write an essay in which you develop your position on this issue. Support your point of view with reasoning and examples taken from your reading, studies, experience, or observations.

3. <u>Essay Prompt</u>:

Consider carefully the following quotation. Then read the assignment below it and plan and write your essay as directed.

"All art is an imitation of nature."
           —Seneca, Roman philosopher, c. 4 B.C.–A.D. 65

Assignment: Do you agree with this statement? Plan and write an essay in which you develop your position on this issue. Support your point of view with reasoning and examples taken from your reading, studies, experience, or observations.

ABOUT THE AUTHOR

Doug Tarnopol brings a unique mix of talents and experience to SparkNotes and the new SAT *Power Tactics* series. He has taught and tutored students of all backgrounds and advised both students and parents in preparing for the SAT. Doug graduated *magna cum laude* from Cornell University in 1992, earning a B.A. in History. He continued his work in the history and sociology of science at the University of Pennsylvania, receiving an M.A. in 1996.

While in graduate school, Doug began teaching SAT test-prep classes. After completing his graduate work, Doug moved to New York City and continued working in test prep, adding PSAT, SCI HI, SAT II: Writing, SAT II: Math, GMAT, and other courses to his repertoire. In 1999, Doug became a curriculum developer, designing instructional material for state proficiency exams.

Doug also writes fiction and poetry. He is an avid drummer, biker, and reader. He currently lives in Metuchen, New Jersey.

SPARKNOTES
Power Tactics for the New SAT

The Critical Reading Section

Reading Passages
Sentence Completions

The Math Section

Algebra
Data Analysis, Statistics & Probability
Geometry
Numbers & Operations

The Writing Section

The Essay
Multiple-Choice Questions: Identifying Sentence Errors,
Improving Sentences, Improving Paragraphs

The New SAT

Test-Taking Strategies
Vocabulary Builder